Beauty Unfolding

"*Beauty Unfolding* is a sincerely inspirational composition of honest stories from the life of a truly empowered woman. It equips the reader with the necessary tools for achieving ultimate fulfillment and gratitude for all that is."

—**Peggy McColl**
New York Times bestselling author of *Your Destiny Switch: Master Your Key Emotions, and Attract the Life of Your Dreams*

"*Beauty Unfolding* is written with a voice that is not only exquisitely genuine, but raw and vulnerable. Kate Waite gives generously from her heart, demonstrating compassion and an undeniable desire to empower us to find the beauty in life, no matter what!"

—**Mary Morrissey**
International speaker and author of two best-selling books, *No Less Than Greatness and Building Your Field of Dreams*

"In *Beauty Unfolding*, Kate Waite shares how she transcended her toughest life experiences in a way that's powerful and inspiring and gives readers a sense of hope. She is a remarkable woman, and I believe her message will touch thousands of lives!"

—**Dina Proctor**
Bestselling author of *Madly Chasing Peace: How I Went from Hell to Happy in Nine Minutes a Day*

"This book is mesmerizing—every time I want to stop reading it, I can't. Kate is a gifted writer, and I just love what I am learning in her book. You will want to read it from cover to cover."

—**Kelly Falardeau**
Bestselling author of *Self-Esteem Doesn't Come in a Bottle*

**Beautiful New Beginnings
After Pain and Loss**

kate waite

New York

Beauty Unfolding

Beautiful New Beginnings After Pain and Loss

Published in New York, New York, by Morgan James Publishing. Morgan James and The Entrepreneurial Publisher are trademarks of Morgan James, LLC. www.MorganJamesPublishing.com

The Morgan James Speakers Group can bring authors to your live event. For more information or to book an event visit The Morgan James Speakers Group at www.TheMorganJamesSpeakersGroup.com.

A **free** eBook edition is available with the purchase of this print book.

CLEARLY PRINT YOUR NAME ABOVE IN UPPER CASE

Instructions to claim your free eBook edition:
1. Download the BitLit app for Android or iOS
2. Write your name in **UPPER CASE** on the line
3. Use the BitLit app to submit a photo
4. Download your eBook to any device

ISBN 978-1-63047-440-9 paperback
ISBN 978-1-63047-441-6 eBook
ISBN 978-1-63047-442-3 hardcover
Library of Congress Control Number:
2014916268

Cover Design by:
Rachel Lopez
www.r2cdesign.com

Interior Design by:
Bonnie Bushman
bonnie@caboodlegraphics.com

In an effort to support local communities and raise awareness and funds, Morgan James Publishing donates a percentage of all book sales for the life of each book to Habitat for Humanity Peninsula and Greater Williamsburg.

Get involved today, visit
www.MorganJamesBuilds.com

Habitat for Humanity®
Peninsula and
Greater Williamsburg
Building Partner

To my husband, Mark:

You showed me unconditional love at a time in my life when I felt unlovable. Through your eyes, my scars became invisible. Our years of love, friendship, and laughter have awakened me to the beauty in life, which has been a light even in our darkest moments. There is no one I would rather spend my life with than you.

To my daughter Chelsea and sons Carter and Cooper:

You have opened my heart and brought me more love than I ever knew possible. One of my greatest blessings in life is being your mom. Thank you for your love and for always believing in me. I love you more than words could ever say.

And to Malala Yousafzai, Elizabeth Smart, Bethany Hamilton, Gabby Giffords, Robin Roberts, Karen Duffy, Amy Purdy, and any other girl or woman around the world who is creating and finding the beauty in her life, even in the midst of great adversity.

Contents

| Beauty Unfolding

Sweet are the uses of adversity, which like the toad,
ugly and venomous, wears yet a precious jewel in his head.
—William Shakespeare

Introduction

In a Single Moment

There is so much about my fate that I cannot control, but other things do fall under the jurisdiction. I can decide how I spend my time, with whom I interact, and with whom I share my body and life and money and energy. I can select what I can read and eat and study. I can choose how I'm going to regard unfortunate circumstances in my life—whether I will see them as curses or opportunities. I can choose my words and the tone of voice in which I speak to others. And most of all, I can choose my thoughts.
—Elizabeth Gilbert

Life can change in a solitary moment. In just a breath, in the blink of an eye, our entire world can come crashing down. Or, in that same moment, we may unexpectedly transcend into a state of joy so profoundly and utterly brilliant that it ignites genius within us.

Every moment holds the potential for inexplicable suffering—or unimaginable happiness. We seldom get to choose which. But while there may be no limit to the degree and frequency of adversities we may face in our lives, there is also no limit to the amount of utter bliss and abundance we can create in our lives—no matter how devastating our circumstances.

I know firsthand how life can change in a single moment. Mine came dangerously close to ending at a very young age. When I was fifteen, I was set on fire from an explosion in my high school chemistry class. In the midst of those terrifying moments, as the smoke and flames engulfed my tiny frame, I had what many would call a near-death experience. I saw my life teetering between two worlds. While I was on fire, I could see myself looking down at my physical body, lying dead in a coffin. My family and friends were at my funeral, surrounding me, overcome with grief and sobbing uncontrollably. How could this be happening? Was my time on earth coming to an end? As I stood looking down at my family, my heart was wrenched in sorrow. I longed for one more chance to tell them how deeply I loved them. I could not leave this world wondering if they would ever understand how much they meant to me. They needed to know I was not leaving by choice.

Suddenly, an angel appeared outside the ring of fire that raged over my body. She smothered the flames with a blanket. My prayers had been answered. A Spanish teacher, Miss Robertson, whose classroom was across the hall, had heard the explosion in my chemistry class. Not knowing why, she opened the hall closet door and discovered a blanket.

Grabbing it, she ran into my classroom and bravely fought the flames that were terrorizing my body. She later told me her actions were a direct response to a voice she heard inside of her, guiding her to run to the supply closet. Without her, I know I would have surely perished in the fire. My classroom was not equipped with sprinklers or fire blankets. I have no doubt in my mind that I was saved by an angel. Now I would get my chance to reaffirm my love for those I cherished so dearly.

However, this rescue came at a cost I could never have fathomed. Although I did not die in the fire, I was entering a whole new dimension of suffering that had previously been completely unknown to me: hell on earth.

Each second that passed felt like an eternity. The paramedics and firemen arrived within minutes. Fortunately, my high school was just down the street from the fire station. As I was rushed through the hallways, I could see the terror on my classmates' faces. I could only imagine how my piercing screams of terror would reverberate for days within the school hallways.

If my conscious mind had any prior knowledge of what I was about to endure, it surely would not have fought so desperately to survive. The paramedics could not give me anything at all for the excruciating pain that ravaged my body. I begged one of them to punch me in the face, anything that would put me into an unconscious state. Although her eyes filled with tears and exuded compassion, she did not grant me my wish.

Upon arriving at the emergency room, medics proceeded to cut off my jeans, which were seared onto my body. As they cut them off, my burnt flesh was also ripped away. It would be five more hours before I was administered any pain medication. Even then, the morphine did very little to ease my pain. My saving grace came when I finally succumbed to exhaustion and was able to fall asleep.

My life still remained touch and go for the forty-eight hours that would follow. Although I did not realize it at the time, my body was filled with toxins. I was at grave risk of dying from blood poisoning. Deep second- and third-degree burns now covered a third of my body. The flames had ravaged my legs and abdomen. My porcelain skin was now a blanket of charred, raw lesions that extended from below my knees, up the front and back of my legs, and onto my stomach. Surviving took on a completely new significance for me. It meant that I would be starting my life over with a body that was not only unrecognizable but also terrifying. Ugliness not only clenched its roots in my body, but in my entire state of being.

Everyone around me knew that it took every ounce of my being to try and comprehend what was happening to me. I could not possibly bear any more than I was already consciously aware of. But even then, I surely would have willed myself to die had I any prior knowledge of the months and years of excruciating physical and emotional pain still ahead.

I was forced to enter a grueling season one often associates with death. Like the harshest of winters, bone chilling and seemingly endless, my body could do nothing other than follow the laws of nature. I could only begin to regenerate new skin and heal after my dead flesh was excavated.

I immediately began the daily ritual of enduring the debridement tanks. Burn survivors often refer to them as torture chambers due to the barbaric, mind-blowing pain they cause. No drug can mask the agonizing pain of having dead tissue scraped off, nor the torture of being left with nothing but exposed nerves. This process took over a month to complete. No amount of wishing could make it end sooner. After this phase was over, I would have my first of two skin-graft surgeries. Thin layers of skin would be shaved from my hips and lower back, and then adhered to the areas where I had third degree burns. This would be the only way my wounds could heal.

Although my physical pain was unimaginable, the emotional hell I faced was arguably as immense, and far more complex. Demons began to overtake my every thought, poisoning my mind with insidious ideas about how I could put an end to my suffering. I began believing that this terrible accident had happened because I was a terrible person. At the time, I could not imagine anything worse happening to an individual, and I couldn't fathom any other possible reason for a human to be forced to endure such torment.

My lengthy hospital stay was finally coming to an end, and I would soon be able to go home. But the life I knew before this horrific accident was already over. Although I had always been blessed to have the love and support of wonderful family and friends, I felt as though I had nothing to live for. Certainly I was never going to live the life that I had always envisioned for myself. Before the fire, my only dream had been to one day fall in love, get married, and start a family.

But one solitary moment had forever changed my life. I was left disfigured, in a body completely foreign to me. Any beauty I thought I possessed was gone, as was any hope that a man would ever love me or that anyone would find anything remotely beautiful about me. I felt like a hideous monster, sentenced to live the rest of my days alone, banished from society. I saw myself as damaged goods, not even worthy of my own love. As I stared out the hospital window, I found myself wishing I had died in the fire. How could I ever find any reason to be happy or grateful about anything ever again?

That's when a stranger entered my room. I normally would be thrilled to have visitors, but on this day, I did not give a damn about seeing anyone. Even as I heard the door open and the footsteps approach my bed, I continued to wallow in my darkness and stare out the window at the adjacent buildings. A woman began to speak softly, her words cutting into me like a knife. "I bet everyone who has come to see you has offered you sympathy. Well, I'm different," she said.

This remark certainly caught my attention. I became enraged at her audacity—how could this woman presume to know anything about me, or what I had been through? I rolled over to lock eyes on this cruel woman. She continued to speak: "I cannot offer you sympathy, but instead I can express empathy. I too was badly burned as a young girl."

Up until this moment, everything I had heard from my loved ones, friends, and even strangers had been kind yet meaningless—because no one *had* been able to understand what I was enduring, both physically and emotionally. She now had my full attention.

I intently listened to her remarkable story. As a teenager, she was severely burned on her back from scalding water. Although our scars were not identical, we both shared the same fears and suffering. Could love, marriage, and children exist for a woman whose body was so grossly disfigured? I was stunned to learn that she was able to move past her doubts and insecurities and live her life to the fullest. She seemed genuinely happy with her life. She told me how she had fallen in love, gotten married, and been blessed to have children. She traveled and did everything she had always set out to do. This woman was living the life she desired—in spite of the terrible adversity she had faced. She had found a way not to let her burns define her.

After she left the room, my eyes filled with tears. In one single moment, my life changed completely—again. A slight breath of life whispered within my soul, *What if . . . What if I could find happiness and create the life I desired?* "What if" turned out to be all I needed to move forward.

When the time finally arrived for me to leave the hospital, I was ready to begin my new life. I knew I would face challenges, but I had found some peace within myself. I never knew the name of the woman who entered my hospital room that day, but I found myself calling her Hope—because that was what she had given me. And I was extremely grateful for this precious gift.

I made a vow to myself, as we were driving away from the hospital, that I would someday find a way to pay my gift forward. My purpose in life had dramatically shifted. Now I was determined to serve others by sharing my gift of hope with those who were suffering from life's most challenging circumstances. Being the painfully shy girl that I was, this thought terrified me. But somehow my fear seemed small in comparison to this new sense of purpose that was much bigger than me. It became an indelible part of me, now woven into my soul.

For now, it was too daunting to think about exactly how I would be able to honor this vow. I would focus on taking one day at a time and allowing myself to imagine *What if. . . ?* After all I had endured, I allowed myself to believe that life from now on would be relatively easy. I didn't know how wrong I was.

Enduring the fire was only the beginning of what would be a thirty-year quest from hell to happiness. It would take years and further cycles of trauma for me to realize that not only did I keep surviving these dark times, but that first gift of hope was only the first of many precious gifts I continued to receive, gifts I perhaps couldn't receive any other way. I've come to call these gifts my GOLD nuggets, and in this book, I'd like to share them with you.

My painful experiences awakened me to a higher level of consciousness. The GOLD nuggets emerged as I became enlightened to a whole new way of being. As soon as I began to add pieces of GOLD to my life, I started to see the ugliness in my life fade into the distance. That's when I began to see the true beauty unfold.

This is not just a story about a girl who found hope after surviving a horrible, life-altering event. It can also be your story of healing and a roadmap to the hidden blessings in the midst of your pain that can transform your life.

If you are living through pain and loss, I can offer you *empathy,* because I have walked down that path. But more importantly, I have written this book to show you that every experience of pain leads to an even greater gift—once you open your mind and allow yourself to surrender to the endless possibilities of joy and abundance available to you. This may seem impossible to believe, particularly when you are ravaged by pain and despair that seems never-ending. But I hope that my story will give you that foundational gift of hope: if happiness is possible for me, what if it's possible for you, too?

The truth is that living a life filled with joy and abundance is not only possible but also simple to achieve. All you need are the right mindset and the right tools, which you will find in the following GOLD nuggets, a trail of treasures along the path of suffering you may find yourself on, likely through no choice of your own. Make no mistake: although the actionable steps are easy to follow, they will require effort on your part. If you are truly hungry for lasting change, you will need to have faith that transformation is possible.

My hope is that *Beauty Unfolding* will completely shatter your paradigm—not only of adversity but also of how you define beauty in your own life. May you open yourself to the possibility that there is beauty hidden in your emotional and physical scars. Understanding how beauty can unfold from pain will allow you to create your own beautiful life, regardless of your circumstances.

Section I

Your First Piece of GOLD

Gifts God Gives
Own Your Actions, Own Your Life
Love Yourself
Dig Deeper

Chapter One

Gifts God Gives

It is this belief in a power larger than myself and other than myself, which allows me to venture into the unknown and even the unknowable.

—Maya Angelou

Our souls' path to full development and enlightenment is much like a seed's path to becoming a flower. A seed is planted beneath dry soil, and it must persevere to push through the dirt. But its ability to push through the soil and grow relies on two important things: the light of the sun and the nourishment of water.

Your soul has the same ability to bloom and flourish as it pushes past the soil of your pain and challenges. It too depends on light and

11

water. For me, the light symbolizes your faith in something larger than yourself, a belief and trust that a higher power exists over mankind. I think of this higher power as God, the Divine, Creator of the Universe, or Spirit—the source of unconditional love and light from which all things are created and possible. The water symbolizes the unexpected blessings that come during your challenges. These buried gifts are simple, pure, and nurturing. They have the power to allow the beauty in your soul to unfold.

With growth, there is pain. However, with growth, there is also the promise of light beyond the darkness. Without struggle, you would never experience the absolute joy of living out your full potential, as you rise above your circumstances and grow in ways you could not have otherwise fathomed.

As I mentioned in the previous chapter, the sheer physical pain from the fire pushed me into a state of shock and gave rise to a single, hideous thought that would not escape my mind: I was a terrible person, and God was punishing me. After all, I had always believed that God was pure love. If I was being subjected to hell on earth, I must have somehow deserved it.

I desperately tried to relive every moment of my life to identify what I could possibly have done that was so awful. I tortured myself with guilt and shame, believing that this would never have happened to me if I was truly a good person and that I must be unworthy of God's love and compassion.

In time, I came to understand that this belief couldn't have been farther from the truth. I was not being punished. Although I was certainly not perfect (nor is anyone, for that matter), I was, in fact, receiving blessings from God that reached farther than I could possibly have comprehended at the time. Admittedly, when I was feeling trapped and scared, I did not see the beautiful gifts that God was sending me. The offerings and blessings came after I was able to surrender to God and trust that the pain and suffering would not last forever. And it did not.

In fact, the years following my accident were filled with many blessings. Not long after I thought my life was over as a result of the fire, I met my best friend and love of my life. Mark and I were introduced when I was nineteen and a sophomore at the University of Massachusetts, Amherst. He had recently graduated from West Point and was getting ready to leave for Officer Training School.

I could not ignore my deep attraction to Mark. His handsome good looks, infectious smile, and the fact that he was a really good athlete could not be denied. I was in awe of the level of commitment, hard work, and intelligence it required to become a military academy grad. It was easy to fall in love with Mark. We had an instant connection, and our love grew quickly.

I was completely terrified to tell him about my accident, fearing that he would see me as damaged goods. But to my amazement, my scars were invisible to him. They seemed to have no effect on his feelings for me; he never once looked at me any other way than with absolute love in his eyes. I could hardly believe it was possible, and at the same time, I was too grateful to question it. What began as hope, after my accident, now became belief. My dreams for my life were beginning to evolve. I was blessed, and I knew it.

Mark and I married two years later. At times our life felt like a fairy tale. We spent the first few years together traveling around the country while Mark raced on the national cycling team. After he graduated, Mark had become a member of the military's world athlete program. His goal was to represent the army in the Olympic Games, as well as in other international events around the world. After Officer Training School, Mark's military orders were changed so he could be stationed at Fort Carson, not far from the United States Olympic Training Center. Within two short years of Mark starting his cycling endeavors, he achieved what many thought to be impossible—he made the 1988 US Olympic team. He was one of the eight men selected to represent the United States in the men's four-man cycling team time trial in South Korea. Although he was officially named as a member of the US team, he didn't get to travel to Korea, as the United States only had four men travel over to the Games to compete. Although it was a huge disappointment for Mark, he had many other opportunities to represent the United States in Europe and Japan and had many successes. Our life was one exciting adventure.

Most importantly, we loved each other deeply and were the best of friends. We had big dreams for our future and believed we could endure anything that came our way, as long as we had each other.

Once Mark had finished his commitment to military service, we decided to settle in Connecticut and start a family. Shortly after, we were blessed with two beautiful and healthy children, Chelsea and Carter. In life few things come close to perfect; but for us, the life that we had created together felt truly amazing. Never could I have imagined that I would be able to experience such happiness in the wake of my accident.

However, as we entered our tenth year of marriage my life as I knew it imploded into a million pieces. Mark, the kids, and I had just returned from a family vacation in Hawaii. Years earlier, my parents and I jointly purchased a home in Maui, and it had become a second home for us. Mark and I had spent many happy times in Maui, both together and as a family. Except this trip was very different. Something was wrong from the moment we arrived. I had never seen Mark so unhappy or, worse yet, so distant. Something was terribly off, but I did not know what was going on. Of course, like any other couple, we had our disagreements from time to time, but we always resolved our issues quickly and were able to move past them. But this time Mark tried to dismiss the obvious fact that something was bothering him. Trying to pry it out of him only seemed to agitate him further. It scared me. In our ten years of marriage, I had never experienced anything like this. I felt helpless and could not imagine what I could have done or what else could be causing him such unhappiness. For the remainder of our trip, I did my best not to pressure him to tell me what was going on.

My mind quickly changed focus on the day before we were set to leave the island: we received word from my brother Michael that my grandmother had passed away. She was my last surviving grandparent, and I had loved all of my grandparents dearly. It was such a blessing to have them in my life for as long as I did. On one hand, I was happy that she was reunited with my granddad in heaven. They had loved one another for over seventy-five years. Yet it broke my heart that she was now gone. Her passing marked the end of an era: the joyful time of having grandparents in my life.

Days after my grandmother's memorial, I was hit with another devastating blow. Mark told me that he could not be married anymore. Not in my worst nightmare could I have ever seen this coming. From my perspective, we were not only best friends, but also passionately in love with one another—even after ten years of marriage. We still shared the same hopes and dreams as a couple and for the beautiful family we had created. I felt completely blindsided.

It felt like another death in our family. Mark moved out a day later. He finally admitted to me why he couldn't be married any longer: it was impossible for him to give me the love I deserved, because he was unable to love himself. His words cut into me like a knife. I desperately wanted to say or do anything to keep him from leaving, but I had to admit that I understood. I had known for years that Mark struggled with many unresolved traumas from his childhood and his relationship with his family, but he would never talk about it. I often tried to get him to open up to me about his feelings regarding his family, but it was one area he never cared to discuss.

I was acutely aware that his unresolved feelings were a ticking time bomb. But I never pushed the issue because I struggled with my own demons. Ironically, we both felt unworthy of each other's love. I had kept my own dirty secrets of shame and deep despair buried inside of me ever since the fire. For years I had been trying to suppress my own feelings of self-hatred. So, although I felt lifeless and heartbroken, I had compassion for what he was feeling.

My children and I became the collateral damage of his dysfunctional upbringing. Although my husband had fought valiantly to ignore his feelings, the war that silently raged within him could no longer be contained. The demons inside threatened his very existence. His abusive childhood and the years of severed ties with his family repeatedly chiseled away at his self-esteem, convincing him that he was not worthy of being loved by anyone, nor deserving of the family we had created.

Although I desperately tried to give Mark as much love and support as I possibly could, I had to come to the painful realization that I could not fix what was broken inside of him. It was clear that he was not ready to get help and face his anguish. It was extremely frustrating to me, because I thought that admitting it meant he was ready to finally deal with his painful past. However, he only wanted to put as much distance as he could between himself and his problems. He was looking to escape. He knew very well he would have to get counseling for us to try to be a family again, so he slipped further and further away.

I made the decision from the beginning that my priority was our children, regardless of what I was going through. They needed me now more than ever. I may not have been able to help Mark, but I certainly would do everything I could to be there physically and emotionally for my kids.

I lay awake at night for hours filled with panic, worrying whether I would be able to provide for our children. Accepting that I could not fix my marriage broke my heart. To have the courage to file for divorce took every bit of strength in my being. It was not what I wanted. However, after months of uncertainty, it was the necessary step to bring some stability to our lives. Mark wanted the best for our children, and also for me. He signed the house over to me, and we settled everything with only one lawyer.

Mark had always been very successful in his career, but I was fearful that his unresolved emotional issues might spill over into his professional life. *Then what?* We had just moved into our new home, and the kids were settling into their new lives. The last thing I wanted to do was to uproot our children and create more instability. But unless I started to bring in my own income, financial hardship was a real risk for our family. I had to find a way to become financially independent.

Determination set in. I would do whatever it took to provide for my children. My babies could not possibly understand why their world was being ripped apart. They were scared and confused and needed my love and care more than ever. The truth was I needed them, too. I often felt either completely numb or as if I were bleeding from the inside out. Both were unbearable. Yet the unconditional love and affection I received from my precious children sustained me through my darkest moments.

I had never been afraid of hard work. In my heart, I was praying that I would be able to create an income from doing something I enjoyed. I needed a positive outlet more than ever. I did not want to just find a job. If I was going to be a working mom, I desperately wanted a career. I knew I had a small window of time to figure it out; I could not afford to wait until it became a necessity. But what on earth could I possibly be qualified to do? This question ripped deep into the very issues that had eaten away at me for years. I had always believed I completely lacked any talents or skills.

I was passionate about design and decorating, but I strongly doubted I was good enough to make a career of it. I would often get compliments from friends who visited our home, and from strangers, about my sense of style, yet I shrugged it off. I thought anyone could do what I did.

At the time, my sister Susie was also at a crossroads in her life. She had recently relocated back East, looking for a fresh start. The timing was right for us to combine our creativity and start our own decorating firm. I knew it would be a risk, but I feared greater consequences if I sat idle, paralyzed with fear.

While planning and preparing to open our design business, a chance meeting on a daytime talk show opened wide a new door of opportunity for us—not as decorators, but as fashion designers (which I'll talk more about in chapter 15). It was ours to take if we were willing to be open to it.

I knew it was the beginning of something really special—and it was. That day, Martha Love was born. We derived the name of our new fashion design company from family names honoring our paternal grandparents, both of whom were incredible artists. Their talents and creativity inspired us to take this bold leap into fashion design.

I was a self-taught designer and marketer, with only raw talent and big dreams. Yet with an extraordinary amount of passion, and a lot of hard work, Martha Love dresses and handbags were sold in upscale department stores and coastal boutiques across the country. Within a year, our designs were featured on *ABC News, Good Morning America,* and *All My Children.* I even had the honor of designing handbags for a celebrity wedding held in the Hamptons.

It was almost impossible for me to believe the changes happening in my life. That I could discover passion, excitement, joy, and success in the midst of one of the darkest, most frightening times of my life felt surreal. One of the greatest and most shocking gifts of all was recognizing, for the first time in my life, that I was a very strong, smart, and creative woman, with talents that were just beginning to unfold. It unleashed a confidence within me during a period of my life when it was a daily battle not to feel worthless.

Here I was in what could only be described as one of the lowest points in my life. Yet, I was discovering blessings I know I would have never received had I not been led down this journey. For the first time since I was burned, I began to seek counseling to work through the years of torment I had kept silently within myself. By trying to block out the trauma I had experienced in my life, I had inadvertently fueled its existence. Although it was no easy task to work through pain I had spent a lifetime running from, it helped me gain perspective and see a bright light within myself, which had been overshadowed by darkness for years.

Facing my past and learning to deal with my new circumstances released me from the prison that had captured my soul. For the first time, I was able to acknowledge the suffering in my life and, more importantly, express the emotions I had buried deep for so long. Doing so was incredibly freeing. I was able to tap into an inner strength and take action to create vibrant change in my life. I found something positive to focus on—my children—and used them as the catalyst for me to move forward. I was finding peace and a whole new way of life on my own. Little by little, I was becoming prouder of the woman I had become and blessed from the unexpected gifts God gives.

No matter how unimaginable your adversity may seem, know there is light on the other side of your suffering. Begin by believing that the possibility to create happiness again does exist. In times when nothing is certain, you are best positioned to discover all that is possible!

Unwrap the gifts.

1. Surrender yourself to accepting whatever hardship, challenge, or loss is present in your life. Release any denial that may be keeping you from dealing with your challenges head on.

2. Allow yourself to experience the pain. As difficult as it may be for you to hear, you will not be able to move past your suffering unless you allow yourself to feel and to work through the raw emotions that have accompanied your experience. Numbing yourself to your hurt will only delay healing, possibly for years. You can never successfully escape the need to deal with your emotions. Trying to flee will only keep you a prisoner to your pain. Choose *not* to succumb to your adversity. Working with a licensed therapist or counselor may be of extreme value to you, especially if you are trying to overcome a trauma. Seek a referral from a physician, friend, or family member who has had success working with a therapist. Never feel ashamed for seeking help; take pride in taking positive action.

3. Open yourself to the possibility of "What if . . . ?" What if God could have a better plan for your life? What if your suffering will result in your discovering something precious? What if you could discover a new happiness you might never have known had you not gone through this transformation? Faith can take you places you may never have dreamed of. The beauty of faith is that you need not know *how* something could be possible. You just need to foster a glimmer of belief that it *is* possible and put your trust in a higher being. God's powers are infinite and transcend anything you could possibly know as a human. Grab onto some faith, and open your mind and heart to "What if . . . ?"

4. Begin to notice the small blessings that may be easy to overlook in your everyday life. Chances are you are surrounded by grace, but if you are drifting in darkness, you may not be able to recognize it. Shine a light on your blessings, such as the

compassion of a friend, the love of family, your health, a job, a roof over your head, or just the companionship of a sweet, furry pet. As you begin to discover the gifts that are already present in your life, you will begin to blossom.

Chapter Two

Own Your Actions, Own Your Life

To the extent that we blame others for any circumstance, even if we believe it to be their fault, we diminish our power to make the changes we are craving to make. Blaming has become the disease of our time. It sets us up to be victims, which then renders us powerless over our circumstances.

—Debbie Ford

When bad things happen, few would ever admit that they enjoy being a victim. Yet so many find themselves stepping into this role whether they realize it or not. Victims blame others, their circumstances, bad luck, the economy, and a slew of other "causes" as the core source of their suffering.

As feelings of helplessness surface within, victims become paralyzed by their circumstances. Overall, it's an extremely dangerous and incapacitating mentality to embrace. I know this all too well, because I had a trial membership in the Victims' Club.

Within days of being burned, I was referred to as a burn victim over and over again, gaining immediate access to a lifetime membership in a club I hadn't realized even existed. Little did I know that there were hundreds, maybe thousands, of other exclusive victims' clubs that targeted millions of others all around the world: "I had a bad childhood." "My husband left me." "I lost my job." "Bad things just keep happening to me." And it goes on and on.

Let me state this very clearly: it is not my intention to show a lack of compassion or empathy for anyone who has experienced something terrible, whether by accident, misfortune, malice, or even his own doing. It kills me to see suffering, whatever the cause. Also, bad things do happen to good people. Your suffering may in truth be a direct result of the actions of someone or something else. However, the danger lies in settling into a victim's mindset.

Allowing yourself to embrace the role of a victim strips you of the power and control to take back your life. In order to fully heal and move ahead, it is absolutely necessary to work through the pain and emotional suffering you endured so you can be free to release it. Holding on to anger and despair will not serve you. It will eat away at your soul and become the ultimate barrier to finding peace and happiness again.

It is natural to feel sorry for yourself when you're suffering. Self-pity may feel like a quick fix to ease your hurt. Yet the reality is that it can have far-reaching consequences that sabotage the rewards available to you. You must recognize you do not need to remain a victim forever.

I am ashamed to admit that I kept my ownership in the burn victims' club for almost fifteen years before I fully grasped this concept. I believe we often keep repeating certain lessons until we gain the insight and knowledge we need to evolve to our next stage of growth. As a soul here on earth, I too had to repeat certain lessons. Only when my marriage started to fall apart did I begin to shift from victim to survivor.

Initially, I blamed myself for the failure of my marriage. I immediately went back to the story that had secretly fed me since Mark and I married. It was the same one I grabbed onto when I first entered the burn victims' club. Because I had been burned in a fire, I was damaged goods, and no one would ever truly love me. Neither Mark nor any man could ever truly see past my scars to the beauty within me. I adamantly believed that one day Mark would wake up and want more than what he had with me—and that seemed to be exactly what had happened. In my mind, the fire robbed me of being a woman who was deserving of love, respect, and admiration.

However, I could not hide from the truth of why my marriage was crumbling. I knew Mark had been silently struggling with hurt that had plagued him for years, well before we ever met. I had witnessed ten years of dysfunction with his family in the time we had been together. Yet I could not prevent the events which were now unfolding.

Extreme anger filled me as I now began to shift the blame squarely on his family for destroying the life I shared with Mark. How could something so terrible and tragic happen to me again? Worse yet, now my children were suffering in unspeakable ways as well. I cried out to God, praying to make it all go away. I had sworn to myself that I was never going to be a victim again, yet here I was, feeling powerless and victimized.

I spent many nights lying awake, nauseated by the horror stories I already knew about women who fell victim to their divorces. More disturbing was that they not only allowed themselves to remain victims for years afterward, but their children also became victims of it as well.

For some, the pain and fear of getting hurt is more than they believed they could possibly bear. I know women who went through divorces and remained lost and hopeless for years. Some gained massive amounts of weight; others swore off ever having another relationship. One was so traumatized she ended up living as a recluse. Sadly, she became so overwhelmed with the failure of her marriage she lost the will and desire to create a new life for herself and her children. Not only did she become a prisoner in her own home, but tragically, in her heart and mind as well.

A part of me would have loved nothing more than to hide under my covers and not come out for days, weeks, or maybe even years. I just wanted my heartache to go away. However, it wasn't a bad dream. The nightmare was real, and it was no longer all about me. I was now a mom. The stakes were much greater than the last time I was tested beyond measure, and giving anything less than 100 percent for my children was never an option for me. Although I did not initially have an exact plan for my future, I did know one thing with absolute certainty: I was not going to become another sad story. For the sake of my children, I immediately had to abandon my victim mindset and launch into survival mode.

The time had come for me to take control of my actions and mindset in order to move forward. It was a huge turning point in my life. For the first time, I had absolute clarity regarding my situation and any hardships that would challenge me in the future. I realized that even when we are faced with circumstances beyond our control, we always have the power to choose how they will affect us.

Here is where you can find great strength and comfort: you can always control your thoughts, feelings, and actions. You may choose to give up your power at times, allowing outside forces to influence your thoughts or behaviors, but ultimately you have sole ownership over them. Only you can decide when you will let go of toxic mentalities and choose a higher purpose for yourself.

Although Mark and I divorced, I stayed true to the one promise I made with myself. I would not allow fear to paralyze me into victimhood. I held my intention to rise above my circumstances and created a happy life for my children, as well as myself. It took some time for me to learn how to be happy as a single mother, as being happy and alone was initially a foreign concept for me. But soon I learned that I could be alone without being lonely. A year after my divorce, I was even able to find the courage to travel to a resort in Mexico all on my own. It was truly out of my comfort zone to do anything of that nature. Admittedly, everyone who loved me thought I was crazy. However, to this day, it was one of the most empowering things I have ever done. It taught me that I could be happy doing anything alone, even one of my favorite things in the world: traveling. If I could travel alone and feel good, I knew I was finally taking control of my happiness.

The single biggest threat to taking charge of your life is not letting go of fear: fear of the unknown, fear of failure, and even fear of suffering further loss and pain. To rise above fear and finally let go of it, you need to recognize that you will never find peace as a victim. Once you decide that you are tired of hiding behind fear and paralysis, you will be able to make the shift to owning your life. You will sacrifice unbelievable happiness if you allow yourself to remain trapped and powerless as a victim.

If you truly desire to escape the prison you are in, it is time to take charge of your life. Decide that today is the day you will take the first steps towards building the life you want to create for yourself. Declare your intentions for the future. Wave good-bye to the victim you're leaving behind, as she disappears in the shadows. Wonderful new possibilities are available for you to discover when you recognize that *you* hold the power to create happiness in your life.

Although Mark and I divorced, our love remained strong. After three years of working independently to heal our past wounds and learning to love ourselves, we found our way back to one another. Our deep love, friendship, and desire to be a family withstood our darkest moments of divorce. We were blessed to remarry in Key Biscayne, Florida, in August 2001, in front of our family and friends. An additional blessing came the following year. Our family received the added joy of welcoming our son Cooper into our lives.

Just as we need to take ownership of our situation when we find ourselves suffering from events beyond our control, we also need to take ownership of our actions and choices that cause suffering for ourselves or others. No one enjoys admitting they made a mistake, especially a terrible one that may have lasting repercussions. However, we are all imperfect beings. We will make mistakes in life. It is an inevitable and essential part of the human experience. Without mistakes, we would miss great opportunities to learn. In fact, some of the greatest lessons we can learn come from the pain and failure we experience when we make bad decisions.

It can be extremely frustrating and disappointing when the one you are angriest with for causing your pain is the one staring back at you in the mirror. Coming to terms with it is never easy. Yet once you can forgive yourself, you will be amazed at how liberated you will feel to move on with your life.

After we had been remarried for three years, my husband and I found ourselves living our dream life in Southern California with our three children. We had been moved out there for business from the East Coast. We quickly adjusted and fell in love with our new life in California. We had a beautiful home and great friends, and we loved our new lifestyle, spending a lot of time enjoying the outdoors. However, about a year later, the company my husband worked for was acquired by a much larger corporation. He had been through several acquisitions in the past, but he was not too happy about this one. He began to question his career and his professional direction heading into the future.

After many long discussions, we decided to start a business together that would provide medical garments to burn patients. A friend, who was more like a brother to me, convinced us to form a partnership with him and his wife. They had already built a successful business as a manufacturer and supplier of medical products, and they would act as our supplier and distributor while we built our own company. Mark and I were excited about this opportunity to give back by offering burn patients a better product to assist with their long healing process.

Once we decided to start this business, we had to make many difficult choices for our family. The hardest decision was to uproot our family again and move back across the country to Georgia so that we could be hands-on in developing our products and building our business. We certainly knew there were risks involved. However, never in our wildest dreams did we expect our partners to deceive us with a web of lies, which would result in losing the lifetime of financial security we had built.

In addition to having all our savings invested in our new venture, we had the rest of our money tied up in real estate. Our partners wanted to make sure we were committed to our new business venture, so they strongly urged us to buy a home in Georgia, "to show we had skin in the game." Going against our better judgment, we purchased a home in Georgia before our home in California was sold. The market had been very strong in California at that time. Within a month of purchasing our new home in Georgia, the market began to crash hard and fast in California, particularly our area of Newport Beach. We decided to rent our house out in California for a year before eventually selling it. As tempting as it was to move back to the place we loved, we were committed to the success of our business. Had we known the truth about their true intentions, we would have sold our home in Georgia and moved back to our beautiful home in California that we still owned at the time, while the real estate market was still strong in Georgia. We could have sold our home in Atlanta for a profit. However, not knowing the truth in our business situation, we decided to stay in Georgia. Consequently, we ended up taking huge losses on both properties as a result of our decision.

If that weren't enough, without warning, our partners pulled out. Let's just say their actions were disingenuous. We had put our blood, sweat, and tears into building the business, creating a large customer base that very much wanted our product, but now we had no supplier or manufacturer. We desperately searched for months to replace them, but we knew that it was going to be a huge challenge since the fabric was proprietary to our former partners.

Put simply, our life was a mess. Because of the constant deceit we had been fed, we ended up making a series of costly, life-altering decisions, which hurt our family immensely. Mark and I couldn't believe that people we loved so much could have no regard for the destruction they inflicted upon our family's lives. We also blamed ourselves for not recognizing their true character and for allowing ourselves to fall victim to their greed and deception. Although our decisions were based on lies, we still had to take ownership of our decision to invest all of our financial security in individuals who were clearly unworthy of our trust and, most importantly, own our decision to ignore our intuition.

We were raw and shaken to the core of our existence. Even though we had the best of intentions for our family and serving others with our business, we were sickened with consequences that we now faced.

Although we could not change some of the circumstances we now had to accept, we were not left without choices. One of the first decisions we made was to move back to California. Although we had been blessed to meet many wonderful people in our community, it never quite felt like home for us. We missed being so far from the coast, but more importantly, we loved living in California. Moving back was the right choice for us—even though moving back to California would mean for the first time in our marriage we would not be homeowners. We were at peace. It was time to begin to heal as a family, rebuild our finances, and move forward in our lives.

The most valuable lesson we learned was that we were not powerless. Initially, the only feelings we saw and felt were pain, devastation, and hopelessness. But once we recognized that we could decide how to move forward and start anew, we began to see the vast opportunities available to us.

Whether your suffering is a result of circumstances beyond your control or your own actions, you can still decide to take control of your mindset and your resulting actions. Although you may have to accept certain truths about your situation, you still have choices. Decide to strip the power from anyone who threatens your happiness or wellbeing. Don't lose another day dwelling on your losses, regardless of their causes. Choose to focus on your blessings, cultivate new dreams for your life, and plan to take action.

Take control of your life.

1. Understand that, even if you have endured unthinkable suffering, you do not have to remain a victim. The choice to free yourself from victimhood lies solely within you. No matter how awful your circumstances may seem, you have the ability to reshape your reality with your thoughts and actions.

2. Focus on the positives in your life, not your losses. Giving energy to loss will blind you to all the opportunities to create happiness and abundance that are already present in your life.

3. Own your power. Embrace and celebrate the fact that you alone own your happiness. Recognize what you can't change, but open your mind to discovering new realities and possibilities. Use this experience as an opportunity to create new dreams and open the door to living a life you truly desire.

4. Write down a clear description of your vision of your dream life. Create a plan of action, and begin taking small steps towards your desired goals.

_____

_____

_____

_____

_____

_____

_____

_____

_____

_____

_____

_____

_____

_____

_____

_____

_____

_____

Chapter Three

Love Yourself

If we really love ourselves, everything in our life works.
—Louise Hay

This may sound like a silly question, but do you truly love yourself?

Loving yourself may be one of the single-most important gifts you could ever receive. Self-love may feel natural and come easily to you if you were raised in a very nurturing and supportive environment with few negative influences or traumas to distort your perceptions about yourself. Or perhaps finding self-acceptance and self-love may be one of your biggest daily struggles. The good news is that even if you have spent your whole life beating yourself up and doubting your self-worth, you can learn to heal the hurt and find love and acceptance within yourself. It will require some patience and effort, but the rewards will be life altering.

I am not very proud to admit it, but for years, I was mean, highly critical, and borderline vicious towards myself. I secretly suffered from a deeply seated self-hatred. My ugly thoughts were a constant source of self-sabotaging behavior. My paranoid ego was tirelessly vigilant, ready at a moment's notice to remind me that I was not pretty enough, smart enough, skinny enough, tall enough, or talented enough. The girl I saw looking back at me in the mirror was so flawed with countless imperfections that I saw little chance anyone would ever really love her. I scrutinized myself relentlessly until I reached the age of thirty. I couldn't understand why others consistently told me that I was my harshest critic; I thought I was merely speaking the truth.

For as long as I could remember, I had carried a heavy burden of shame and guilt within me. After the fire, I came to believe that my inability to love myself was directly related to this occurrence. My insecurities were on steroids after my accident. Feelings of self-loathing, shame, hatred, and disgust became imbedded into every cell of my being. I became imprisoned by my thoughts. Although being badly burned in a fire certainly played an enormous role in my self-loathing, it was not the sole cause of my suffering. The truth was that I had struggled with a lack of self-confidence ever since I was a little girl.

Shortly after Mark and I began dating, I became haunted with sickening memories of being repeatedly molested as a six-year-old girl. If this had truly happened to me, how could I have completely blocked out such a horrific event from my memory? Yet I soon realized it was most definitely not a figment of my imagination. In one solitary moment, I was able to remember every heinous second of what had happened to me, in vivid detail.

My dad had become a cycling coach and mentor to some teenagers who worked at my parents' bicycle shop. Realizing that some of these guys were dealing with serious family problems, he and my mom would step in and offer their support, often going out of their way to help however they could. My parents would drive them to races, since they did not have cars or rides to get there on their own. Many times these guys would be invited into our home to stay for dinner. My parents had absolutely no idea what was going on behind their backs. They would have never dreamed that any one of these boys would have hurt their young, innocent daughter in such a vile way. Looking back, that is probably one of the reasons I was too terrified to tell them at that time. Of course, as a six-year-old girl, I was emotionally powerless to protect myself. However, the abuse left me with feelings of unworthiness and blame that I buried within myself for years.

I did everything I could possibly do to avoid the toxic secret I held. For years, not even my husband knew the gut-wrenching pain of self-loathing I carried inside as a result. Ironically I was blind to his self-loathing—until our marriage collapsed.

Mark and I loved each other with all of our hearts, yet neither of us could independently love ourselves. And sustaining love in a relationship is impossible if both people do not begin with a healthy, loving relationship with themselves. Mark realized this for himself when he told me, "How could I possibly let you love me, when I do not even love myself?" But as devastated as I was to hear these words, they also awakened me to the bitter deception I also held within myself. Even after ten years of marriage, I was still plagued with my own inability to love myself. I too could no longer run from the monster that captured my soul when I was just a child. It was time for each of us to face our inner demons.

Specifically, it was time for me to seek counseling, if for no other reason than to be healthy for my children. Fortunately, it took very little time for me to decide that I also wanted to get better for myself. I had grown weary from running and trying to escape my pain. I had tricked myself into believing that running from my pain was the quickest way to escape it, but I had learned the hard way that I could never outrun my pain. The path to end one's suffering starts first by acknowledging personal pain. Then you must take action by working through the source of your painful emotions.

As souls, I believe we enter the world as pure light, untainted by hatred, bias, shame, abuse, failure, or any other negative attribute. Only when we begin to live our human experience do we become vulnerable to these qualities. At an early age, we begin to absorb the feelings and thoughts of others around us, and these experiences and events gradually start to mold our perceptions of ourselves.

If over time we are exposed to negative, hurtful, or abusive surroundings, these experiences will likely create insecurities and doubts within us. Deep wounds may even cause us to question our worth as human beings. The more severe and frequent your exposure to these negative influences and circumstances, the more likely you will suffer from low self-esteem. The core of our internal suffering in any circumstance is often linked to negative influences we may have been subjected to early in life. Abuse (verbal, physical, and/or sexual), criticism, failure, abandonment, and trauma can all play a role and be an impetus for self-loathing.

If you have experienced repeated negative messages or traumatic events, especially during childhood, you too may have distorted images and beliefs about your true self. Misplaced blame, guilt, shame, and self-hatred can become your close companions if you do not take the time to do the work to uncover the truth surrounding your pain. In order to return to a place of self-love, you must work on healing your soul.

This process will likely bring to the surface uncomfortable feelings and unresolved issues from your past. However, it is absolutely necessary for you to break free from your negative self-image and learn to love yourself once and for all. Seeking help from a licensed therapist in order to work through traumatic issues can greatly assist you in your healing. Have patience and faith, knowing that if you are willing to do the work, it will clear the way for your light to shine brightly.

If you do not lovingly take care of yourself, you are sending a message to the world that you are not worthy of being treated well, whether it's through addictions (drugs, alcohol, sex, food, etc.) or not caring for your personal appearance, your home, or anything else that is a reflection of you. When you love yourself and are able to show everyone that you value yourself and are worthy of respect, you will set the bar for how others should act towards you. You will become a magnet for all of the good and positive rewards you want to attract into your life.

As a woman, and especially as a mom, I became extremely good at putting the needs of others above my own. So good, in fact, that there was a time when I ceased to believe I was entitled to take any time for myself. It has always been my personal joy to give towards the happiness of others. It is second nature to me. However, my selflessness became unhealthy and borderline toxic when I allowed it to sabotage my own personal happiness and wellbeing. I had to learn the hard way that giving too much of yourself can be detrimental if you have nothing left to sustain your own needs. I unwittingly became a martyr, which only fueled the disgust within myself. Once I was able to learn to love myself and value my significance and worth, I was able to gain a clear perspective on the matter. Loving and giving of myself to help others helps fuels my existence, so it is imperative I maintain a healthy balance of caring for others and caring for my own needs, taking time to nourish my own mind, body, and spirit. Even with the best of intentions, you will have nothing to give to anyone if you do not remember to care for yourself.

If you are having trouble believing that you are worthy of your own love, perhaps a first step may be to realize that you are already worthy, valued, and loved by God. Know you were not dropped into this world by mistake. A divine, loving God created you. You are a soul made from the purest love, created into human form.

Also, remember that your circumstances do not define who you are. They are merely events that have happened. Your authentic self is the core of who you are. It is constantly guiding you on your path, directing you to serve your divine purpose on earth. You are capable of shining your own light if you have the courage to discover your authentic self. This authentic self does not submit to the self-defeating voices or negative influences that may have tainted your original ability to love yourself. Sabotaging yourself with constant criticism, judgment, or misplaced blame will keep you from living your most beautiful life. Discovering your authentic self is your key to creating a life in which you can serve your highest purpose as a loving, giving, generous soul, contributing your gifts and talents alongside others.

Discovering your authentic self will free you to be able to love yourself again just like when you were a small child. Remember, you were born with a natural ability to love yourself by design. Self-love is innate to your spirit. When you are living out of your authentic self, loving yourself is effortless and pure. Self-love only becomes challenging as you're exposed to negative influences or events. When you are able to peel back the layers of hurt and judgment to uncover the source of pain, you will begin to excavate your authentic self and view yourself in a truthful light.

The first step to learning to love yourself is practicing kindness towards yourself. Look at yourself in the mirror and begin by telling yourself that you are worthy of love. Start by accepting yourself as a perfectly imperfect human being, just as each of us was created. Be patient with yourself. The process of learning to love yourself will require effort on your part and time to heal. Have faith, knowing that great rewards will come from doing the work to rediscover self-love. My husband and I are both perfect examples of this.

After our divorce, we each began the arduous process of working through our previous traumas, allowing ourselves to heal and learn how to find self-love. I admit it. It was work. It took several years of counseling, and the desire to create lasting change, before we were ready to be fully available to each other in a committed, loving relationship. Fortunately for us, we had a deep love and friendship at the core of our relationship before we divorced. We were able to remain friends and commit ourselves to continue to work together as parents for our children. After three years, we were blessed to find our way back to one another—now truly free to love one another because we had learned to love ourselves.

Make today the day you begin to love you.

1. If you have been struggling with addictions or suffering abuse, make today the day you choose to set yourself free with the truth. Please reach out to a loved one or close friend, or call a community helpline, to take your first steps toward getting the immediate help you need. Even if you are incapable of seeing how you can rise above your situation, have faith that it is possible. With the right help from a doctor or licensed therapist, and a willingness to do the necessary work, you can overcome even the most challenging circumstances.

2. Learn to recreate your inner dialogue. Begin and end each day with reciting positive, uplifting affirmations to yourself. You can create your own or use affirmations created by others that will help you see yourself in a loving, kind, and positive light.

Below are some examples that may lift you up as you begin your transformation.

- My worth is not defined by my circumstances or how others have treated me in the past.
- I am priceless. There is only one of me.
- I am a child of God (or our Creator), made in His image, capable of greatness.
- I accept that I am not perfect—no one is. I love my perfectly imperfect self, even with the flaws I have.

    Make a commitment to recite affirmations like these two or three times a day for the next thirty days. Every time a negative thought about yourself enters your mind, replace it with a new, positive affirmation.

3. Begin to create a list of things that you love about yourself. Write down as many things as you can think of. It can be anything, as long as it is positive. (If you cannot yet identify anything you love about yourself, start with something you like about yourself—even something as simple as, "I like the way I look in blue.")

    Read this list over to yourself before you get out of bed and again before you go to sleep. Each day try to add something new. Even if it initially seems impossible, once you get started, it will become easier to do. You may surprise yourself and discover new and exciting qualities about yourself that you never noticed before.

1. _____

_____

_____

2.

3.

4.

5.

6.

7.

8.

9.

10. _____

_____

_____

4. Think of ways you can honor yourself each day. What activities would renew your spirit, enhance your mental and physical wellbeing, and light an inner glow within you? If this exercise is a challenge for you, start by scheduling ten minutes for yourself, three times a day: once in the morning, once in the afternoon, and once in the evening. Close your eyes and take several deep breaths. Clear your mind and only allow thoughts to enter that are centered on your own peace and happiness. When you are done, write down any inspiring thoughts that can be implemented in your life. Remember, caring for yourself will not only sustain you, it will allow you to be more present and available to give to others.

_____

_____

_____

_____

_____

_____

_____

_____

_____

_____

_____

_____

_____

Chapter Four

Dig Deeper

Character cannot be developed in ease and quiet. Only through experience of trial and suffering can the soul be strengthened, vision cleared, ambition inspired, and success achieved.
—Helen Keller

When you are faced with challenges or adversity in your life, do you have a silent confidence that you will, in fact, overcome your obstacles? Or do you tend to feel hopeless and powerless, readily throwing your arms in the air and surrendering? For a lengthy period of my life, I certainly felt void of courage, and I greatly underestimated my own inner strength.

Countless times after my accident, people would tell me that I must be an incredibly strong person for enduring the trauma I had been through as a burn survivor. My knee-jerk reaction was to completely disregard these comments. In my mind, I never had a choice in the matter. I had merely been placed in unfortunate circumstances, where I had no alternative but to deal with my fate. I believed I had neither strength nor courage. But I was completely wrong.

It would take almost fifteen years for me to discover a deep well of endless inner strength. It was readily available to me, patiently waiting for me to tap into it. All I had to do was choose to accept it.

In the early days after my initial separation from Mark, I sank into a black hole. I felt weak, helpless, and terrified to be alone. How I could possibly survive yet another unexpected, heartbreaking trauma? If I survived, I was certain that I would never fully recover. Surely I would languish in incomprehensible grief until my dying days. But, after a brief period of indulging in self-pity, I began to regroup and chose to own my power.

It was time to let go of my debilitating thoughts. For the first time, I began to acknowledge the incredible courage and mental fortitude I already possessed. I was an incredibly strong woman. I had not only survived a horrific accident, but also found the courage to rise above my adversity and create a new life for myself. I remembered that defining moment after the accident when I had to decide whether I would fall to my knees and surrender, or get back up fighting harder than ever. I decidedly opted for the latter. To do that surely required strength.

This memory summoned me to take a look back at my life and delve into other experiences that had tested my character. How did I handle adversity before? As brutal as my life had been at times, I had found ways to endure and move on. To my amazement, I had far surpassed my previous expectations of simply surviving awful events; I was able to discover more happiness than I could ever have fathomed. The truth was that by the time I hit adulthood, I had a cache of life lessons, which

I could recall to bolster my inner strength. I just needed to dig deep within myself to unleash it.

However, an ongoing battle with my self-confidence often clouded my ability to tap into this strength. During these times, when I needed further resources to muster my resilience, I turned my attention elsewhere to the everyday heroes I saw around me, those who defied the odds to overcome tremendous hardships. When I struggled to dig deep for strength on my own, I found it far easier to look towards others for inspiration.

Each and every day, average human beings are doing extraordinary things. Major news and media outlets rarely tell these stories, because they would rather incite fear with dark, often gruesome headlines. Seldom do they share stories of hope, faith, or triumph over adversity. Yet millions of people accomplish miraculous achievements daily.

Your strength could be inspired by anyone, even those you have never met personally. It could be your next-door neighbor, whose bravery extends far beyond his combat time in Afghanistan. Now missing one of his legs, his previous life no longer exists. Not willing to succumb to his injuries, he created new dreams for himself. Further exemplifying his enormous courage, he recently celebrated crossing the finish line in his first marathon, only months after adapting to his new prosthetic.

Perhaps you find empowerment from the beautiful ten-year-old girl in your child's class. She lights up a room with her infectious smile, even though she has lost all of her beautiful hair from countless rounds of chemotherapy.

Or maybe it comes from a local family where last year both parents were out of work due to layoffs. Now they are on track to significantly increase their combined income by deciding to take a chance and start the business they always dreamed of owning.

As for me, three incredible women not only greatly influenced me, but they also became the source of my determination and perseverance.

Of these women, the closest to my heart is my mom. She showed me firsthand the depths of her fortitude.

My mom has always been the rock in our family and is no stranger to adversity. She experienced countless situations while I was growing up that could have broken her. My dad was a cyclist and longtime bike racer. Always passionate about cycling, he would occasionally compete in bicycle races while I was growing up, and it was always a family affair. But one fateful day nearly shattered our family. It was a day I will never forget.

It was a seemingly perfect September morning. My dad, my brother Michael, and I left early in the morning to head to the race. It was a special day for me, because I was going to get to spend some time alone with my dad. We usually did things together as a family, but today my mom and sister stayed home. Mom was busy preparing for company, which was expected to arrive later that day.

Things went horribly wrong when my dad went down in a crash during his race. Fortunately, I did not see it happen. A family friend came to inform me that he fell but assured me he was okay. He had a headache afterwards, so a friend drove us home. My dad tried to downplay the severity of his injury and did not even go to the hospital until hours after he arrived home. What started out as a bad headache ended up being a fractured skull and a blood clot on his brain. My dad was immediately hospitalized, and within the week, his condition became grave as he slipped into a coma. He remained in a coma for several days. It was touch and go, but by the grace of God, he survived.

His recovery was lengthy and required him to undergo surgery. At the time, my parents had owned and operated a local bicycle shop. Although its existence relied heavily on my dad's daily presence, somehow my mom managed to step in and keep it running smoothly, all the while tending to my dad's extensive recovery and caring for three young children. Thankfully, he was able to make a full recovery, but he had a very long road of healing ahead of him. Two brain surgeries and months of healing were not only traumatic for him, but for our family as well—especially my mom.

While under that much stress, a natural inclination may have been to hide, locked away behind closed doors, wallowing in self-pity. Not my mom. She remained calm and in control, reassuring us that we would be okay.

I truly believe that in some small way this experience helped to prepare her for the shock and horror of what I had to endure. I can only begin to imagine the terror that ran through her body as she received the call telling her I had been burned in a fire at school. How could something this tragic happen at school?

As a parent, there is no greater pain than helplessly to watch your child suffer. Although I know many times she was overwhelmed with her own suffering, she singlehandedly brought me more comfort than anyone else could. My mom and I were always very close, but after my accident, our relationship became unbreakable.

She was the first face I saw when I arrived at the local hospital. After many hours there, the doctors had me relocated to St. Barnabas Burn Center. I can honestly say it was my mom's love, strength, and constant support that got me through the hell I endured. She made the daily two-hour drive to the Burn Center and spent the majority of each day with me. She remained by my side for the two months I spent in the hospital and for the grueling years of healing I faced later. Through many tears and even some laughter, I got through it. I have no doubt that my mom is the reason why. In my most difficult hours, she was my greatest gift. It took this tragic situation for me to recognize one of the greatest blessings in my life: my mother's never-ending love and devotion to me. It was always there; I just did not know its depth.

My mom's ability to remain astoundingly patient, nurturing, and loving during the most terrifying times we faced as a family gave me the courage to know I could do the same. She and I will be forever bonded from this experience, which grew from previously unimaginable circumstances.

The second of these women who never ceased to inspire me is our sweet neighbor, Elaine Meluso. She was not only a neighbor, but also a dear friend to my mom. Elaine's husband had passed away at a young age after a battle with cancer. She became a single widow raising three small children, one with severe Down syndrome, when she was only in her thirties. If that were not enough to bear, her youngest child also developed leukemia, and then Elaine developed breast cancer. If you were to meet Elaine, you would have always been greeted with her warm smile and genuine concern for others. She would seldom mention her problems, but instead chose to focus her attention on the blessings she had in her life. Elaine ended up losing her daughter from complications of her illness. Elaine continued valiantly to fight on. Her own cancer was aggressive, and she fought numerous types for over twenty years. Her greatest wish was to see her two children happily married and to become a grandmother. With faith, absolute resolve, and God's grace, she lived long enough to fulfill her dreams. To this day, Elaine lives on in my heart as a constant reminder that everyone has the power to choose to live a beautiful life—regardless of his or her circumstances.

I would feel disingenuous if I did not pay honor to another astonishing woman who greatly influenced my life: Oprah Winfrey. Never could I have imagined the indelible impact she would have in shaping the woman I have become. As a teenager and through my adulthood, I came to know her as a light in my life. Although we came from two very different worlds, I recognized early on that we both had endured tremendous adversity growing up. Yet here was this amazing woman who boldly crossed over all types of barriers and stereotypes to create a life filled with purpose, serving others. She surpassed all odds and never gave up. Instead, she took action on her dreams and placed tremendous faith in God.

It was never her status as celebrity that inspired me. It was her authentic desire to help others grow, love, and forgive in ways they may never have thought possible. Her example is a constant reminder for me also to never give up. In my most desperate hours, I find solace and courage from her unbreakable will and fierce determination.

May you find inspiration from these determined individuals who not only overcame great challenges and hardships, but who also exemplify the unbelievable rewards that are available when you dig deep within yourself. Remember, some of our greatest leaders, visionaries, and humanitarians have had to overcome some of life's most challenging adversities in order to reach their ultimate successes. The same may be true for you.

Dig deeper.

1. Take a moment to close your eyes. Then take several slow, deep breaths. When you are feeling relaxed, try to remember a time in your life when you were able to achieve success by digging deep to find your inner strength. Maybe it was a significant achievement, or maybe it was just a small hurdle you were able to get over. Be especially mindful of any events that seemed difficult to overcome but you got through anyway. Take a few minutes to reflect upon this memory. Use this as a tool to remind you of the power which you hold.

2. If you are struggling to rely on your own ability to survive and thrive, look towards an outside source for some help. Do you have someone in your life you value and trust? Ask her to cite

incidences when she may have seen you demonstrate strength or bravery.

3. Create your own list of people who have overcome incredible odds and have achieved great success. Think of as many people as you can. Who has inspired you in your life? What obstacles or great challenges did they rise above? Write down the names of your own personal heroes and the personal struggles they overcame.

_____

_____

_____

_____

_____

_____

_____

_____

_____

_____

_____

_____

_____

_____

_____

_____

_____

_____

_____

_____

_____

Section II

Your Second Piece of GOLD

Gratitude
Omit Negativity and Limiting Beliefs
Learn to Forgive
Ditch Perfection

Chapter Five

Gratitude

Develop an attitude of gratitude, and give thanks for everything that happens to you, knowing that every step forward is a step toward achieving something bigger and better than your current situation.

—Brian Tracy

essons on gratitude have elevated my soul and allowed me to experience more joy than I could ever have believed possible. Boundless gifts become available to you when you experience a deep sense of gratitude. Ironically, gratitude will often rise to the surface from your darkest moments. At times, gratitude may seem impossible in your current situation and mindset. Pain and loss can sink you to the bowels of hell. They will not only test your limits, but they will also force you to examine closely yourself and the life you are living. Any painful or negative events that occur can blind you from seeing anything good that may already exist in your life.

After being burned in the fire, I was consumed with feelings of loss; I absolutely believed I had nothing to be grateful for. Initially, my physical and emotional pain, coupled with my extensive physical scars, blinded my ability to see anything beyond their awful existence. I could not even feel grateful to be alive. It seemed as though everything had been taken from me, leaving me emotionally and physically bankrupt.

Not long after I had been released from the hospital, I had to return for my first outpatient visit. As I walked into the waiting room, I came face to face with other burn survivors for the first time, and my heart sank with shame and heartbreak. For the first time, I saw how incredibly fortunate I actually was. Some had lost limbs or their eyesight. Most gut wrenching were those who had lost their identity; severe burns had melted their entire faces away.

I felt as though someone had just punched me between the eyes. I truly did have a reason to be grateful beyond words. Granted, my circumstances were still very painful and presented their own share of challenges to overcome. But realizing how much worse it could have been gave me a starting place for understanding authentic gratitude and embracing it. It allowed me to move forward.

During the days immediately following the collapse of my marriage, I would find myself drawing upon this defining moment in my life. Once again I felt as though my life was ending, at least the only life I had come to know and love. Having anything else less than a loving marriage with our children seemed unbearable to me at the time. I desperately searched for any reason to want to continue moving forward in my life—other than for the sake of my children. I loved them dearly, but at the time, I hated my life.

astly, I was extremely
for. My day was not
on the blessings I
resent in your
ays you feel
oments of
w small
do the
enge
ns

; given an

e book *Simp*

d all of the ill-

ide. It powerfully rem

desire in life to feel gratitu

ide does not depend on how

nd in the *simple abundance* that

simple joys already present in my

lessings and gifts to me that I may not

nizing the gifts already present in my life did not

me struggle. One of the first exercises suggested in

dance is to make a list of five things each day that you're

for. During such a dark time in my life, this exercise seemed

possible to do. Yet, I was desperate to find any reason to be grateful, so I decided to give it a try. Tucked in bed and mentally exhausted, I began to recall every moment I experienced over the course of my day. Initially my mind focused on all of the things that had gone terribly wrong. It took most of my strength just to get through the events of my day.

But then, to my amazement, I remembered something wonderful that had happened. It was so simple and sweet, yet undeniably powerful; it got me through the day. It was a hug and kiss from my children and hearing them tell me they loved me, which brought me great comfort and joy. For this, I certainly was grateful.

There it was: a beginning. I now had a seed of gratitude planted that now could grow. Within minutes, more positive thoughts began to enter my mind. I was happy and grateful for the sunshine that I felt on my face on such a cold winter's day. I appreciated the call I received from one of my dear friends, who wanted to let me know she was there for me. I was grateful for the fact that my lovable little dog, Lulu, was

...side, bringing me comfort. And ...my children were safe and well cared ...bad as I first thought, once I chose to focus ...ad along the way.

As you become aware of the little blessings already ... life, your life will also begin to transform. Even on the ... completely beaten down, try to come up with just three ... your day you're grateful for and write them down (no matter h... or insignificant that moment may first seem). Then tomorrow, ... same. Keep doing this every day for at least three weeks. Chal... yourself, as you go along, to come up with even more than three reas... to be grateful and write them down. Once you make this part of you... daily habit, chances are you won't want to stop. This extremely powerful exercise may be the key to your journey of abundance. When you begin opening your mind and heart to discover how much you already have to be grateful for, you are preparing yourself to receive even greater gifts of abundance.

Live in gratitude.

1. So, go ahead and ask yourself: today, what are three small (or big) reasons to feel grateful? You may be surprised to discover the blessings already present in your life.

1. _____

_____

_____

_____

2. _____

_____

_____

_____

_____

_____

3. _____

_____

_____

_____

_____

_____

2. Start a gratitude journal. As you begin the process of discovering your hidden blessings, write them down daily. Recognizing your current gifts and abundance will help you feel empowered and give you momentum to find strength and move forward.

3. Take several moments each day in silent meditation or prayer to express gratitude for all of the gifts and blessings in your life. The more you feel and express gratitude, the more abundance will flow into your life. You will be amazed at how quickly you receive more once you begin to appreciate all that you already have.

Chapter Six

Omit Negativity and Limiting Beliefs

All that we are is a result of what we have thought.
The mind is everything. What we think, we become.
—Buddha

In times of despair, it is often challenging to release negative thinking and limiting beliefs. It becomes particularly difficult to maintain a positive attitude when, as a society, we are bombarded daily with fearful, demoralizing, and often hopeless thoughts and images. All you have to do is turn on the news or go online to be blasted with one horror story after another. It seems as though the world has gone crazy and is spiraling madly out of control. You are consistently being sent the message that *life is hard*, and *hurt* and *suffering* are part of normal, everyday existence.

Quite frankly, this way of thinking is not only detrimental to your wellbeing, but it is also extremely toxic. Of course, bad things do happen, but that in no way means your life has to become a reflection of them. Your thoughts will shape and create your reality. If you hold on to fear, negative thinking, and limiting beliefs, your world will be built on these pillars. That means your foundation will be weak and susceptible to faults and cracks, making you more vulnerable to falling and crashing down. A foundation of fear becomes a barrier to the life you want, making it much more difficult for you to achieve the goals you desire or dreams you hold in your heart.

However, if you focus on positive thoughts, have confidence in your abilities, and can rationally distinguish between legitimate and imaginary fears, you will be able to build a strong foundation that will produce positive outcomes in your life. Your mind is singlehandedly the strongest, most powerful tool you have to create lasting change in your life and achieve the positive results you desire.

Unfortunately, many have had negative messages and disparaging tapes playing over and over in their heads ever since they were small children. If this was true for you, you have unknowingly become conditioned toward a fearful mindset, which hinders your ability to go after your dreams.

For example, you may have heard the following damaging beliefs repeated time and time again: "Life is hard." "You will never be wealthy."" You are not smart enough, pretty enough, or thin enough." "Marriage is hard work." "You will never amount to much." "You always get sick." "You are a disappointment." "You will never do it." And on and on it goes. Even if these damaging beliefs resulted from misguided attempts by loving parents or family members trying to protect you, they will have negative consequences. You must learn how to break free from these destructive thoughts. Otherwise, they will become a self-fulfilling prophecy; you will create your reality based upon what you believe to be already true for yourself.

In Rhonda Byrne's powerful book *The Secret*, she refers to this theory as *the law of attraction*. The law of attraction means that you will manifest the things in life your thoughts give the most energy to. It suggests that anyone can have the ability to receive whatever he desires— once he learns how to tap into the unlimited abundance available to him from his own subconscious mind. When this book reintroduced readers to this ancient principle, it created a worldwide phenomenon. It shattered the self-imposed barriers many individuals held. People began to discover that in order to attract what they desired, they needed to release their own limiting beliefs.

The good news is that you do not have to remain trapped behind detrimental thoughts and beliefs embedded into your subconscious. You hold the power to change old patterns and break this cycle by not allowing adverse thoughts into your mind. With practice and a concerted effort, you can begin to reshape your thought patterns by replacing destructive thinking with clear, positive, uplifting thinking within your psyche.

By the time I reached adulthood, my head was continuously swarming with ugly, debilitating beliefs about myself that were sabotaging my happiness every chance they could. I had always thought of myself as an extremely honest person, but the truth was that I had unconsciously been telling myself lies for years. I convinced myself that I was only being a realist, but there was nothing real about the gross distortion of my flaws and ill-conceived judgments I formed about myself. It was as if I was looking at my reflection in a trick mirror, which could never portray an accurate view of the woman I was.

I only became aware of my dysfunctional behavior as I began to step into my role as a successful designer. From time to time, I had received compliments on my great style or flare for design, but I would quickly dismiss these compliments, telling myself they could not possibly be true. Yet here I was, launching a line of women's dresses and handbags, designing, operating, marketing, and successfully selling to upscale department stores and boutiques. Not only did this amaze me in and of itself, but I was also doing it as a single mom. It was time for me to own the truth about myself and let go of the garbage that had been holding me back. I could finally admit that I was extremely capable, creative, smart, strong, and yes, talented. This awakening became an incredible gift—one I could only receive from myself. I was finally free to become the woman I was always capable of being, but never confident enough to embrace.

Overcome your limiting beliefs.

1. Are you allowing negative thought patterns and limiting beliefs to hold you back in life? It is never too late to break this cycle. Begin today by changing negative thoughts into positive ones. Every time a limiting belief arises in your mind, quickly replace it as follows:

   I am not_____. Change to:
   I am_____.
   I can't_____. Change to:
   I can_____.
   I will never be able to_____ Change to:
   I am able to_____.

2. Are your negative thoughts real or created out of fear? Are you holding onto someone else's limiting beliefs that have been imposed on you? *Do not allow* others to limit the greatness you are capable of achieving. Living in accordance with these

negative beliefs will hinder your ability to live your life to its fullest potential.

Think of any limiting and negative beliefs that others may have imposed upon you. Choose no longer to accept them as fact, and release them from your belief system. Create new, positive thoughts to replace them when they arise in your mind. Write down some positive phrases you can use to replace your negative thought patterns.

_____

_____

_____

_____

_____

_____

_____

_____

_____

_____

_____

_____

_____

_____

_____

_____

_____

_____

_____

_____

Chapter Seven

Learn to Forgive

Forgiveness is a gift you give yourself.
—**Author Unknown**

Learning to let go of anger and find forgiveness can be one of the most difficult lessons we face as humans. Our natural instincts teach us to become defensive, angry, and hurt when someone acts in a way that brings emotional or physical harm to us. Releasing the anger, pain, and emotional suffering inflicted by others can challenge us to the core of our being. Yet learning to forgive is essential to creating authentic happiness. Harboring anger and resentment will only add to your loss and suffering. True happiness can only return when you forgive the person who has hurt you. Forgiveness is a gift you give to yourself, not to the person who needs to be forgiven.

Some people have the ability to forgive quickly. Others may struggle to forgive, believing that "forgiveness" means "excusing bad behavior." In actuality, forgiveness means letting go of the past so you can live fully in the present.

One of the challenges of forgiveness is to recognize that person who hurt you can no longer harm you once you strip the power away from him. Learning to forgive has been a reoccurring theme in my life. It has taken me numerous life lessons truly to understand the power of forgiveness.

Admittedly, I am one of those people who wears her heart on her sleeve. As much as I often wish I could conceal my emotions from others, I never have been very good at hiding my feelings: good, bad, or otherwise. So, if I am hurt, there is a pretty good chance the person who hurt me is going to know it. Many times, this emotional transparency has presented a chance to clear the air and move forward. If my feelings were justified, an apology would often follow. If I felt the apology was sincere, that was usually all it would take for me to forgive. For years I believed that if someone genuinely asked for forgiveness, you should grant it. In other words, I understood forgiveness to be a gift we give to the other person in exchange for an apology.

As a result, I began to think I was a pretty forgiving person. This illusion lasted until I was faced with having to forgive someone who lacked any remorse or desire to be forgiven. How could you possibly forgive someone who did not ask for forgiveness?

This posed a great challenge for me. I thought I had a real handle on forgiveness—until I found myself becoming a prisoner of the past. I knew I had to move on, or else my past would rob me of my happiness in the present. At times the hurt I was holding onto caused me to ache physically. It had become deeply rooted within the walls of my body. Its vines wrapped around my insides, squeezing so tightly that at times it hurt just to breathe. The pain became unbearable. I wanted desperately to forgive and move on, but I became trapped by the lie that I could only forgive and move on when the other person showed remorse for his actions.

Finally, it dawned on me: why was I continuing to relive this horrible hurt, over and over again, when the person who caused my pain wasn't thinking about it at all? Once the incident was in the past, I became the only person responsible for allowing myself to continue to hurt. Why allow myself to miss out on one more moment of happiness? At that moment, everything became crystal clear. The weight and heavy burden of the chains I had been carrying were lifted off of me instantly. I possessed the key to free myself all along, yet I was clouded with false truths that only existed within my ego. My higher self always knew this to be true. Once I quieted my mind and sought the truth from inside my soul instead of my mind, the truth revealed itself to me. I became enlightened to the purpose and the immediate gifts that come from forgiveness. I could feel my soul sing with delight. This awakening brought with it more joy than I could have fathomed. Inner peace and happiness cannot exist without true forgiveness. Truly, forgiveness is a gift we give ourselves.

Unleash the chains with forgiveness.

1. Recognize forgiveness is a *gift you give yourself.* Forgiveness will free you to be truly happy and to let go of the pain from the past. Forgiveness does not mean that you are letting the other person off the hook. It simply empowers you to *live fully in the present.* Understand the events of the past can no longer hurt you, because they are now only memories. Each second of each day brings with it every opportunity to create happiness and peace. Become fully present in the moment.

2. Is there someone you need to forgive but you're struggling to move past your hurt and anger? If it is a relationship you no longer want to keep, take a deep breath, and let it go. It will not serve you to hold on to any anger or hurt. Look yourself in the mirror and remind yourself that you are forgiving the other person so he can no longer hold any power over you. *You own your happiness*, and you're not going to allow him to take another second of it away from you. Feel empowered and at peace. If the other person truly has remorse, he will have to live with the consequence of his actions. If someone has truly inflicted pain and suffering on you and refuses to acknowledge his poor behavior, do not waste another moment of your life dwelling over it! His actions will most likely catch up with him sooner or later. Most importantly, why would you fill your thoughts and give up your own happiness over someone who does not value you or your feelings?

    However, if you value and desire to continue having a relationship with the individual who has been the source of your suffering, let him know of your feelings. You can either choose to speak with him or to write him a letter, expressing that you value your relationship and would like to move forward. Do so without the expectation that you will receive an apology or a show of remorse. Once you have expressed your feelings in a non-confrontational way, release any lingering anger, hurt, or sadness you may have been holding on to. This is the *gift you give yourself*. To genuinely move forward, you cannot live in the past, because you can never go back and relive it. You cannot live in the future, because no one can have any certainty about his or her future. The present is all that truly matters. Be mindful of this and live fully in the present.

Chapter Eight

Ditch Perfection

Nothing important, or meaningful, or beautiful, or interesting, or great ever came out of imitations. The thing that is really hard and really amazing is giving up on being perfect and beginning the work of becoming yourself.

—Anna Quindlen

I spent years trying to create something I could never attain: perfection. Human beings are not intended to be perfect. We are all perfectly imperfect. From our imperfections, flaws, and mistakes, we learn great lessons in life. Yet, we are constantly bombarded with messages from society suggesting that perfection does exist. Our fears and insecurities fuel the belief that perfection can be attained. But it is an illusion.

Admittedly, in my quest for perfection, I have become quite familiar with my imperfections throughout the years. My preoccupation with my flaws and perceived deficiencies only distracted me from discovering all of the gifts and talents I possessed.

A year and a half after Mark entered the corporate world, we moved into our custom-built dream home in Connecticut with our beautiful daughter Chelsea, who had just turned one. We had wanted to live by the coast but settled into the quaint little town of Brookfield. Although it was not on the coast, across the street was a lake. Brookfield seemed like a charming place to raise a family.

Mark had received a degree in nuclear engineering from West Point and was working in Stamford for a company that traded uranium. Earlier in my pregnancy, I had made the decision to hold off on a career, because designing our home became a full-time job. I know it was the right decision for me at the time, but it still came with its own set of consequences.

After the newness and excitement of moving into our new home wore off, we began to focus our attention elsewhere. For Mark, it was simple. He would transfer his drive and determination from his cycling career and apply it to his aspirations to climb the corporate ladder. For me, it was not quite as easy. I loved being a stay-at-home mom and cherished the time with Chelsea, but I often felt invisible. So, I decided to become the perfect suburban wife and mother. As ridiculous as that sounds to me now, it made absolute sense at the time. Marrying young and forgoing a career path only added to my insecurities. Other than being a great wife and mother, I could not fathom any other way I could be of value and feel as though my contributions in life mattered. Little did I know, I was setting myself up, trying to become something that was impossible to achieve.

Frankly, it was delusional for me to aspire to become some type of trophy wife on a multitude of levels. However, I had convinced myself that if I could become the wife who would make my husband proud (especially at corporate functions), while also raising the perfect family and living in a perfectly kept home, I could overshadow all my other imperfections that haunted me daily. As much as I tried to enjoy the many blessings in my life, I was obsessed with the fear that one day I would lose everything. This fear would haunt me for the next five years.

Trying to be a perfect wife and mother would have been exasperating and impossible for anyone, but it was especially so for a woman who viewed herself as irreparably damaged. If nothing else, I was hell-bent on at least trying.

I gained a ton of weight when I was pregnant with our daughter and then, a few years later, with our son Carter, but I was fortunate to have been able to lose the fifty-five pounds and almost seventy pounds I gained with each of them. I was petite, five feet tall and weighing around a hundred pounds through most of my adulthood. Even though I was my ideal weight for my height, I was never satisfied with the reflection I saw in the mirror. I had always wished I could be at least five foot ten. That would be the perfect height. Shortly after Mark and I began dating, someone commented that we would look like a model couple if I were only taller. For years it killed me. I could do nothing to change this glaring deficiency I hated about myself. So I was rarely happy with the way I looked, even though I made certain to keep up my appearance at all times. I often overdressed because I wanted to look like a professional, even if I was a stay-at-home mom to our two small children. I silently dreaded going to business functions with my husband because I was so fearful of how the other women would view me.

Unfortunately, my insecurities carried over to my parenting skills as well. I worked overtime making sure our kids behaved and looked like model children. Since I was lacking any positive self-image, I looked to them to reflect upon me in a good light. They were often complemented on their polite manners and on how nicely they were dressed. This gave me some slight comfort, thinking that I was responsible for creating that. But it was only one small way I could feel validated. I also was responsible for the look and feel of our home.

We were extremely blessed to live in such a beautiful new home. I took on the responsibility of making certain that it continued to look like a model home, even after living in it for several years. I would vacuum the carpets daily, making sure you could see the marks left behind from the vacuum. I frequently would take an old toothbrush and get down to scrub the grout on our kitchen floor with bleach, so it looked brand new. There was never anything lying around or out of place. The kids always picked up their toys and put them away when they finished playing. It honestly did look like a model home on a daily basis. Unfortunately, I allowed myself to believe my worth was somehow based on how well I performed these tasks.

After almost five years of living this way, I was sinking deeper and deeper into my black hole. I loved my family dearly, but I hated myself. I was completely empty on the inside. To make matters worse, we had not been happy with our decision to settle down in the town that we chose. Although it was charming, it was not for us. We felt alone and disconnected from being part of a community. I was quietly dying a slow death. The truth is we both were, for many reasons. So, we made the extremely difficult decision to sell our dream home and move to Westport, where we both knew we belonged. As hard as it was to give up our beautiful home, we were eager to move on.

It took almost a year for us to sell our home, so we were more than ready to leave when it sold. Chelsea was five and Carter had just turned two. We knew we were not going to have all of the comforts of our previous home, which was fine with us. We would be happy with any home as long as it had charm. To our amazement, our wonderful realtor, Marilyn Heffers, found us the perfect home, right off of Turkey Hill. It exuded charm, from the meandering brook and waterfall in our front yard to the beautiful hardwood floors and oversized fireplace in the living room. We fell in love with it and made an offer right away. It had an outdated kitchen and main bath, which was actually perfect, because we could add a few custom touches to our liking. We moved in that summer, starry-eyed about our dreamy new beginning.

My life seemed surreal. Never in my wildest imagination could I have fathomed that we could be living in this lovely town, a few blocks from the sound and down the street from . . . *Martha Stewart*. I loved Martha. My family would jokingly call me "Martha," because, in some ways, I wanted to emulate her. To me she seemed perfect. She is beautiful; she is the ultimate entertainer and decorator; and she knew how to live her life beautifully. From my earliest memories, I had always been passionate about living beautifully. I have always wanted to reflect that passion in every area of my life. I shared an appreciation for her classic style and could very much relate to her vision to create beauty in everything that surrounded her.

Living in Westport definitely surrounded me with beauty—at times more than I could handle. For the first few months we lived there, my insecurities rose to a new high. I became so self-conscious and insecure over what others would think of me that I was afraid to venture out. Everyone around me seemed to be living the perfect life—or so I thought.

Once I learned to relax a little, I began to love our new town and became a little more comfortable in my own skin. To my surprise, we quickly settled in, meeting wonderful new friends who were completely down to earth.

We were fortunate to be able to do a complete kitchen and bath remodel a few months after we moved in. I loved the design process and enjoyed creating new things. It is something that I have always been passionate about. It was incredibly exciting to see our home take shape. For a short while, my life began to feel as close as you could get to perfect. For the first time, I began fully to love my life.

And then the bubble burst. The perfect life I believed I was desperately close to attaining blew apart in an instant. Within seven months of moving to Westport, our marriage fell apart. The initial shame I carried with me was overwhelming. We were on the cusp of living the perfect life. How could this be happening to me now?

I did everything in my power to hide my separation from my husband from as many people as possible. My hope was that I could fix my marriage before I would ever need to tell anyone that it was holding on by a string. I put on my big-girl panties and a smile and tried to pretend everything was great. This facade came crashing down a few weeks later, when a nosy neighbor began sharing her suspicions about the whereabouts of my husband. Although I was furious at the time, she ultimately did me an enormous favor. Hiding and pretending nothing was wrong was quickly taking its toll on me. It was exhausting. I needed to focus every bit of my energy on taking care of my family, not to waste it playing games.

Admittedly, I did not expect the reaction that followed. I received love and support from my new friends I had made in town. There were no judgments. They genuinely cared for me.

One of the most shocking truths I discovered came from a close friend of ours. After he learned of the inner turmoil my husband was facing, he said, "I am in total disbelief. I thought Mark was Superman. He had it all: good looks and the perfect wife, family, and job. I thought, *There is a guy who has the perfect life* . . . I can't believe it!" I was shocked by what I was hearing. He thought *we* had the perfect life? I was incredulous. Yet for the first time I began to understand how we often allow our own insecurities to create an illusion about other people's perfection that in reality does not exist.

How often do you see a woman or a couple who seem like they have it all, yet you have no intimate details of their personal lives? They could have challenges and pain invisible to others, yet very real to them.

Comparing yourself to anyone is pointless. I learned this lesson the hard way, through a gut-wrenching divorce. I can never be the perfect wife, mother, daughter, sister, friend, or woman. I can only strive to express the best version of me.

The same is true for you. Recognizing perfection is an illusion will eliminate a tremendous amount of pressure and wasted time. Focus on having pride in yourself for giving your best, knowing you did just that. Regardless of your circumstances, it is absolutely possible to live a beautiful life—once you open yourself to the beauty in your life that already exists.

Let go of perfection.

1. Start noticing the beauty in imperfection. Look around you and begin to recognize anything imperfect that you still love or admire. Focus on its positive attributes, not its flaws.

2. Do you expect perfection from your loved ones, friends, or others you admire? The answer, most likely, is no. Stop setting unrealistic standards for yourself that you would never have for others.

3. Give yourself a break! Once you let go of trying to be perfect, you will unleash a wave of freedom. You will gain the confidence to become more adventurous, without being paralyzed with the fear of failure. It is okay to make mistakes and, at times, even fail. You'll be better equipped the next time you try. The greatest achievements and successes come from individuals who do not let the fear of failure hold them back.

Become the best at accepting your flaws and knowing your strengths. Don't worry about being perfect. You're human, it's simply not part of your DNA.

Section III
Your Third Piece of GOLD

Grieve and Say Goodbye
Open to Change
Let Yourself Shine
Discover Your Passion

Chapter Nine

Grieve and Say Goodbye

There is an art to grieving. To grieve well the loss of anyone or anything—a parent, a love, a child, an era, a home, a job—is a creative act. It takes attention and patience and courage.
—**Elizabeth Lesser**

L etting go may seem like an impossible task to many. But the laws of nature make grief and loss inevitable. Everyone will experience it at different points throughout his life. Grieving is not only necessary part of healing, it is a healthy way to move past your suffering. It is crucial to release any pain from your past in order to find joy and happiness in the present.

I was blindsided the first time I had to come to grips with great loss. After being burned in the fire, I had no choice but to accept this

77

bitter reality, and nothing could have prepared me for it. My innocence had already been taken from me as child, and now I was being robbed of what little childhood I had left. It was as though I had to become an adult overnight. To add to my devastation, I inhabited a body that was not only terrifying but also inescapable. For a very brief period, while I was still in the Burn Intensive Care Unit, I convinced myself that any physical scars I now had could be magically erased by a skilled plastic surgeon. However, I learned very quickly that my loss was permanent. My body would heal. However, I would be left living the rest of my life with scars covering a third of my body. This was a lot for a fifteen-year-old girl to absorb, much less accept. Prior to my accident, I was a perfectly healthy young girl.

For a long time, I did everything in my power to hide from the dark pain that existed deep within me. I carefully concealed my scars from the outside world. I would avoid having to see my scars in a mirror at all costs. It petrified me to acknowledge my loss. Doing so would force me to face my suffering.

Not until I was mourning the end of my marriage was I able to finally come to terms with my scars left from the fire. Once I faced my hurt, I was able to allow myself to grieve. It was liberating to know that a physical death is not the only loss to merit grief and that I was entitled to grieve. Any substantial loss one feels is reason enough to grieve. Grieving opens the doors to healing. Crying and releasing sad, negative feelings is therapeutic. It will free you to accept what you cannot change and move on.

Five years ago, I went through another dark period of mourning that lasted for nearly a year. I experienced the sudden and unexpected end of two relationships with friends whom I loved dearly. Although I was not related to either of them by blood, they each felt like siblings to me. Each loss was devastatingly painful and the fact that they came within months of each other only made the experience more unbearable. However, the circumstances and the gut-wrenching emotions I experienced with each could not have been more different.

Bruce was like a big brother to me. We met when I was just eight years old; he was thirteen years my senior. My dad became his mentor and coach, paving the way for Bruce to pursue his cycling passion and ambitions. He would often spend weeks at a time staying in our home. My mom would always roll out the red carpet to make certain he felt like a special member of our family. He was never made to feel like an extended guest.

Through the years our relationship did evolve into *family*. There was never a time in which he was not included in a family event. Our family grew even closer through extended relationships that included our spouses and children. I thought Bruce and his family would be part of our lives forever—that is, until he destroyed our friendship with the ultimate betrayal. Bruce and his wife were the friends we trusted as our business partners. And their dishonesty cost us dearly.

Their actions were so insidious we had no choice but to cut them out of our lives immediately. The death of our relationship was instantaneous. Mourning the loss of our friendship and the love we had for them was another matter. Time was needed to heal our wounds and find the strength to move on.

The emotions we felt were raw. It was not easy walking away from someone whom for years we loved so dearly. Yet we knew it was necessary for our own happiness. We had to forgive, heal, and forge ahead, which helped us learn from this lesson. We knew we had to let go of resentment in order to be free to be happy again.

Karen, on the other hand, was one of the most beautiful souls I ever met. She had light brown hair and a beautiful smile. She had an inner radiance that made anyone in her presence feel like he was being wrapped in the warmth of the sun. We met after we had settled into the same neighborhood in Georgia and became best friends almost instantly. It was as though we had known each other for years. She was one of the kindest, sweetest, most giving women I have known. At times, she lacked confidence in herself, yet she had a silent strength that was easy for others to recognize. She was always completely authentic and never allowed her insecurities to change her. Everyone who met her instantly fell in love with her. I only had the blessing of Karen's friendship for about two years before she passed away.

It all happened so fast. She had not been feeling well for a few weeks, and then, after a night of unbearable pain, she was admitted to the emergency room. The next day, doctors confirmed she had pancreatic cancer. She passed away three weeks later. Those who loved her felt some solace in the fact that she did not linger for months on end, suffering in agony. Nevertheless, the pain of losing this beautiful human being at only forty-eight years young was immense.

Death felt as if it had become anchored inside my body. In time, that feeling began to dissipate. Sadness over Karen's passing took an unexpected turn. I would always miss her dearly. However, I found myself incredibly grateful for the gift she was in my life, even if for only a brief period of time.

Something else extraordinary began to happen. As I came to accept her passing, I started to feel her presence around me from time to time. Once, when I was having a particularly bad day, I could actually sense her presence around me. I remembered once hearing from a spiritual adviser that anyone can connect with spirit. All you had to do was to ask the spirit to show you a sign that she is with you. At first, I was somewhat skeptical. On one hand, I had no doubt that souls never really leave us when they die; only their bodies leave the physical world. I believed that our loved ones' souls remain close by our side, ready whenever we need them. But I was skeptical about our ability to receive confirmation about their presence.

I decided that I wanted to know the truth, and I was going to make the confirmation extremely challenging to manifest. I wanted there to be no doubt in my mind that it was indeed Karen who was communicating with me. I knew that it would take a miracle for her to deliver what I was asking, but it was the only way I would know for certain.

I waited until I could be alone and in a quiet, calm place. I wanted to be clear in my mind and intentions when I had this conversation with her. It went like this: "Karen, I am sure you know how much I miss you dearly and often think of you. I think I can honestly feel you around me at times, especially when I need you most. I desperately want to confirm that what I sense is actually you, not a figment of my imagination. If it really is you, please send a blue butterfly to me. I know how rare they are, but if it is true you can send me a sign, just by me asking, then I guess anything is possible. I will patiently wait for you to respond. After all, I know my request would require a miracle to happen."

A day passed, and I was beginning to second-guess my request. Maybe I was being unreasonable. I should have asked for something more realistic.

The next day I walked into my kitchen and almost fell over. I could not believe what I was seeing. On my counter was a box of computer ink that my husband had just purchased. Right on the front of the box was a picture of a blue butterfly. It was certainly not the blue butterfly I was anticipating, flying in my garden. However, it was a blue butterfly— exactly what I had asked for.

I wish I could say that was the only proof I needed, but I wanted more. Although, it seemed nothing short of miraculous, I wanted to be one hundred percent sure. Again, I sought a quiet place to be alone and speak to Karen. This is what I said: "Karen, to my amazement I saw the blue butterfly today, just like I requested. There is nothing more in the world I want to believe than that was actually a sign from you. Please forgive me for still having any lingering doubts. Would you please send me one more blue butterfly, so I will never again doubt that you are sending me a sign that you are with me?"

Later that night, I decided to buy a book on the new e-reader I just received from my husband for Christmas. I was so excited to get it, since I love to read. Karen and I both shared this passion; she was a voracious reader herself. It had been a while since I last picked up a book. I could not wait to find an interesting book to read. I did not even know where to get started. I decided just to allow myself to explore and see what piqued my interest.

As I began to scroll through the books, I saw a title that looked interesting. I clicked on the title to learn more. On the cover was one large blue butterfly. As the tears began to roll down my face, I noticed the author's name. The author had the same last name as Karen.

I will never doubt Karen being with me again. I regularly see blue butterflies in the most random places. It is usually when I miss her most. This is true of my other deceased loved ones. They show me signs as well. I smile when I frequently see 10:24 on the clock or 8:14 (those are my grandmothers' birthdays.)

If you are interested in learning more about what happens to loved ones after they die, there are many great books out there. One of my new favorite books is *We Don't Die: A Skeptics Discovery of Life after Death* by Sandra Champlain (Morgan James, 2013). The author was a skeptic herself, and after doing years of research, she too is a firm believer that our loved ones remain with us after they die.

Take the first steps toward working through grief.

1. Give yourself permission to feel your loss. In order to heal, you must first acknowledge the pain you are experiencing. Running from it will only prolong your grief.

2. Allow yourself some time to be sad. Crying is a healthy way to release your feelings. Saying good-bye will help give you closure so you can begin to let go.

3. Seek counseling or support groups to deal with any loss that seems overwhelming. Experienced counselors can provide the guidance you may need to cope with your grief.

Chapter Ten

Open to Change

Insanity: doing the same thing over and over again, expecting different results.

—Albert Einstein

I f you are struggling to find beauty in your life, yet you are unwilling to make changes, you too will continue to get the same results in your life. Now I have two big questions for you: Do you readily embrace change, or does change secretly terrify you? How willing are you to step out of your comfort zone and come face to face with your fears?

If you are unhappy with your life, you need both to *accept* and *make* changes. Like loss, change is an inevitable part of living. All forms of life go through change. Without change, life forms would remain in a constant state, and there would be no growth. Change happens—even if you wish to remain stagnant.

Fear of failure or the unknown often stops many from taking action. But it is critical to alter your course if you are to break out of current circumstances. You cannot expect to continue down the same path and not end up at the same destination you did before. Change can seem scary at first. However, once you embrace change and the positive results that are available, you learn to let go of the fear.

You already have much more courage than you realize. At this point in your life, I am sure you have looked fear in the eye many times over. I also bet you have had many successes in your life because you were brave enough to take action. How many of these acts of bravery apply to you: going to school for the first time; making new friends; joining a group activity or sport; going on dates; having a job interview; traveling somewhere new? I would imagine that you've successfully done at least several things on this list. Chances are a few of these things seemed scary to you at first. Your desire to gain a pleasurable result surpassed any fear you may have had. You chose to rise above your fears in order to get what you wanted.

In the same way, you always have the choice to take action towards your goals. Remaining unhappy because you are afraid to make necessary changes is also a choice. *Only you* can decide whether you want to fester in your own misery or be bold and open yourself to change. That may seem harsh, but it is the truth. Why would you rather commit to a life of unhappiness? Positive change brings with it the possibility of experiencing more peace and joy than you could have ever fathomed.

How badly do you desire progress in your life? Is there something you have always dreamed of doing, but your fear of failure kept you from going for it? Maybe you convinced yourself that being with your guy is a better option than being alone. Perhaps you stay stuck in a job you hate just because it is easier than looking for a new career option. Or perhaps you've always dreamed of living in another city or part of the world, but you've been too scared to step out of your comfort zone. Unless you are willing to open yourself to change and begin to take action, your deepest desires will never manifest. They will forever remain a dream.

Not long ago, I had to make a life-altering choice. Did I want to continue to act like a victim, letting other people or circumstances dictate the direction of my life, or was I willing to make changes? I had a very clear picture of what my dream life looked like: I wanted to write a book and share my message to inspire women and girls to live beautifully. Yet, I had become paralyzed with fear. Going after my dreams would require me to be bold, and the changes I needed to make terrified me. I have never been short on having BIG DREAMS, but my lack of confidence and fear of the unknown often kept me from trying. I did not want to put myself out there and end up failing. After all, who wants to put her heart and soul into something, only to fail?

I began to recount all of the times in my life that I took a chance and was bold. In the eighth grade, I tried out for a singing part in our school's production of *Charlie Brown*. I thought I would be perfect for the role of Sally. After all, I was a petite blonde, just like her. Unfortunately, it did not exactly go as planned. No one had bothered to tell me that it was not a great idea, since I am actually tone-deaf. I also attempted to try out to be a cheerleader on several occasions. Apparently, you have to be coordinated to make the squad. I certainly would be remiss if I did not mention my junior prom. Although I was asked to prom, I politely declined. I wanted to go to the prom with a boy that I had a secret crush on. I decided to be incredibly bold and take the initiative to ask him myself. I was extremely shy, so this required me really to put myself out there. The only way I could find the courage was to call him on the phone. I asked to speak with Mike and mustered the nerve to ask him to prom. To my horror, I realized that I had misdialed the number and asked some random

Mike to prom. He was polite and apologetic. I guess he sensed how embarrassed I was. The next day, I found out the guy I wanted to go to prom with was already asked by another girl. She had asked him a week earlier.

One would think after my failed attempts in high school that I would never again want to put myself out there. However, this was not the case. I took chances and was open to any change that I perceived would bring more happiness to my life. I moved for love, took chances on new careers, and even made bold decisions when my life was changing in ways I did not like. Yes, there were even more failures. Actually, they weren't failures at all. They were incredible opportunities to learn invaluable lessons that would greatly benefit me. They were exactly what I needed to experience, at exactly the right time. I am so grateful for all of my experiences, good and bad. They have made me the woman I am today.

Being open to change has awakened me to new possibilities that I may not have ever imagined possible. I have made the conscious choice not to let fear get in the way of me going after my dreams. As terrifying as writing this book, speaking, and sharing my message seemed at first, what I feared even more was coming to the end of my life and realizing I had never tried. What if I had the chance to inspire women around the world to live their most beautiful life—and I didn't take it? Everything I have experienced along my journey has led me to this moment.

So, let me ask you: are you interested in making a change(s) in your life…or are you committed to making change(s)? At first glance, you may be wondering, what is the difference between being interested in change and being committed to change? *Interest* is something that piques your attention but does not inspire action. You merely are entertaining the *idea*. When you *commit* yourself to achieving a goal, you are setting the intention to *do* whatever it takes to reach it—regardless of the sacrifices or any necessary action it requires.

Be bold and commit to change.

Do you have dreams or desires in your heart but are afraid to take steps to go after them? If fear is stopping you, ask yourself, "Is it rational?" Are you willing to accept defeat and perhaps never experience the new possibilities that may exist for you?

1. Take some time to think about all of the things you love about your life. Now think about the things that drain you and bring you unhappiness. What are the small changes you could make to add more joy to your life? Write them down.

_____

_____

_____

_____

_____

_____

_____

_____

_____

_____

_____

_____

_____

_____

_____

_____

_____

2. Now is your chance to be BOLD! What are some bold changes you could make that could put your happiness quota through the roof? Imagine that you cannot fail. What would you want to do to create greater happiness in your life? Write it down. Ask yourself, "What would I have to change in order to achieve my desired results?"

_____

_____

_____

_____

_____

_____

_____

_____

_____

_____

_____

_____

_____

_____

_____

_____

_____

_____

Chapter Eleven

Let Yourself Shine

Our deepest fear is not that we are inadequate. Our deepest fear is that we are powerful beyond measure. It is our light, not our darkness, that most frightens us. We ask ourselves, who am I to be brilliant, gorgeous, talented, fabulous? Actually, who are you not to be? You are a child of God. Your playing small does not serve the world.

—Marianne Williamson

Our spirit desires to shine brightly because it comes from divine light. Yet our human experience has conditioned us to set limits on the amount of love, success, and achievement we feel comfortable attaining. Fear of failure is one reason we hesitate to allow ourselves to shine. This will cause us to sabotage ourselves, leaving us unable to rise to our greatest capabilities. However, the real reason many of us do not step out and shine is because we are too frightened to step into our full greatness. It is success, love, and admiration that we fear most. Everyone has set limits for the amount of good things he allows to come into his life. When we reach these thresholds, our tendency is to shrink ourselves and not fully express the person we are truly capable of being.

One of my first memories regarding public humiliation occurred when I was just three years old. As a quiet and extremely shy preschooler, my mom thought it would be a good idea for me to take ballet lessons. My mom learned that our neighbor was a ballet instructor who had set up a studio in her basement to teach dance classes. I was so excited to wear a pink leotard and tutu. My pretty pink attire overshadowed my nervousness of having to go to her house for lessons.

My mom was not allowed to stay for my class. This terrified me all the more. I never ventured far from my mother's side. I felt safe knowing she was in control.

As far as I can remember, things were going pretty well with my first class. Although I was scared to death to be there alone, I just wanted to follow along so no one would look differently at me. I kept trying to pay attention to my instructor and keep up with the others. Yet I could not ignore a terrible distraction. At first, I tried desperately to ignore it, but then it completely took over my thoughts. It tortured me until I could not take it for another second.

And that's when it blew, just like a dam opening up. My bladder hit its breaking point. That's right. I peed all over the middle of her dance floor. I thought, *If I just keep dancing, maybe no one will notice.* I prayed for another distraction. Maybe someone would get sick and throw up, or start to cry. Then the puddle of pee would not seem nearly so bad.

Well, things did not exactly go as planned. My teacher noticed. Everyone in the room noticed. All of a sudden the ridiculously shy girl, who was so afraid to speak up and get her teacher's attention, had exactly that—her undivided attention! My teacher freaked out. She began screaming at me for not speaking up. The worst part was that she yelled at me in front of my whole class. I had always worked very hard to be a *good girl*, at home and certainly in public. I was ashamed and humiliated at what I had done. Unfortunately, it was just the beginning of the shame and humiliation I would endure throughout my childhood and into my early years as an adult.

To put it mildly, shining brightly had never been one of my goals when I was young. For as long as I can remember, I have always felt extremely uncomfortable when receiving any compliments. It felt completely unnatural for me to think of myself as being relevant. I certainly shrunk away from any opportunity to stand out or be recognized favorably. Growing up, it was the men in our home who stood out for their accomplishments. Following my mom's lead, my sister and I had the role of supporting their successes. It never felt like a burden. We were genuinely very proud of them. After all, I certainly did not feel at ease in the spotlight. I was much more comfortable knowing I was doing my part, while blending in the background. In my mind, there was no reason for me to shine.

After I married, I willingly chose to give a hundred percent of my effort to supporting my husband's endeavors. I believed that if he was happy, then I would be too. Of course, that was not always the case.

One of the blessings that came from my divorce was discovering my authentic self. Before the divorce, I would have argued that I knew exactly who I was. I was a wife, mother, daughter, sister, and friend. I had my beliefs, likes, and dislikes, as well as a firm understanding of my capabilities (or lack thereof). The only problem was that much of what I thought was true about myself was not true at all. It was an illusion created by my own ego.

My true journey of self-enlightenment began as my marriage ended. Being stripped of my identity as a wife left me questioning who I really was. Initially, I wholeheartedly believed that I was nothing without Mark. Being a single mom made me feel as though I was a failure. I felt as though I was a disappointment to my family and, most of all, myself.

Amazingly, something wonderful began to happen. As I started to come to terms with my circumstances, I began to accept and see myself in a whole new light. Establishing a career played a significant part in my healing process. It allowed me to unearth the real me. I discovered my inner being that was free of lies and distorted truths. I found a place where my ego could no longer be in control.

However, deciding to become a working mom was still nothing I had ever envisioned for myself. I was raised with the belief that being a great mom meant being a "stay-at-home" mom. It had been ingrained in me: only out of financial hardship should a woman choose to work outside of the home.

I actually spent an entire semester at college sharing my thoughts on this subject with my psychology professor. I volunteered in a daycare center. Most of the children there came from single-parent homes. I would write about my experiences with the children and how I interpreted the impact their moms' working had on them. At the time, it seemed black and white to me. Either you were a good mom and stayed at home, or you were selfish and sacrificed the needs of your children to fill your own needs. I could not wrap my mind around the concept that it was okay to choose to work outside the home.

After my divorce, and upon realizing my financial situation could change drastically at any given moment, I went into survivor mode. I knew that I no longer had the luxury to rely on others. It was time for me to be one hundred percent responsible for taking care of my children and myself. I owed it to them to do my best. In time, I would understand that I owed it to myself as well.

Now my only decision would be the career path I would take. I always loved being able to express my creativity. Doing so never felt like work for me; it made me feel alive. Although I lacked confidence in my abilities, I decided to focus on what career would make me the happiest.

Being in survivor mode opened my mind to endless possibilities. I spent every waking moment thinking of ways that I could improve my situation. Then my sister Susie had the opportunity to design a dress for a cohost on *The View* (which you'll hear more about in chapter 15.) We had to move quickly to take advantage of this amazing opportunity. In a very short period, we had to design a line of dresses, find fabric suppliers, pattern makers, labels, packaging, and a manufacturer. In addition to what we knew about design, we had to become experts at marketing as well. When we started, we had no idea how we would figure it all out… we just knew that somehow we would.

Becoming a designer was completely out of the realm of anything I would have imagined possible for myself. Other than being creative, I was convinced that I lacked all necessary skills to become a fashion designer, much less the skills required to own our own company. In 1998, the Internet was nothing like it is today. Very few resources were available online. We had to figure out every detail on our own.

My sister Susie had been sewing for years and was an excellent seamstress. This became invaluable since she quickly had to teach me how to sew. We began sewing dresses ourselves on my dining room table.

That determination to "find a way to make it happen" turned out to be our greatest strength. Not only did we make it happen, but we also exceeded our wildest expectations!

In the blink of an eye, my life changed forever. Susie and I had allowed ourselves to shine. It was probably the first time in both of our lives that we let go of our doubts and limiting beliefs. Without reservation, we allowed ourselves to be free to be our true selves. Once again, I discovered that I had been duped by my ego for most of my life. I did not have to live my life in the darkness, dimming my soul's natural light. I was meant to shine, just as every other soul on earth is meant to shine too.

The gift I received from this challenging time was one of the greatest blessings I could ever imagine. I discovered the real me, my authentic self. The years I spent cowering from my own light were finally over. I emerged a whole new woman. I came to understand that my reluctance to shine did not come from my fear of failure; my deepest fear was actually allowing myself to step into my own light. It frightened me to think that becoming my greatest self might make others around me feel uncomfortable. I could no longer accept this way of being. There would be no turning back.

From time to time, I still have my insecurities about my abilities. But now I know without a doubt that sharing my gifts and talents with others is part of my divine purpose. Everyone has been given a reason to shine. It is our natural right to be our brightest being.

For example, two years ago, after all of our losses in Georgia, I wanted desperately to step back into my light. However, I was struggling to move forward. I had been hurting for so long that I had lost touch with my true self. I had bold dreams but lacked the courage to pursue them.

It may sound funny, but Katy Perry is the one I have to thank for inspiring me to shine again. The first time I heard her sing "Firework," tears started streaming down my face. It was as though the song was written for me to hear. Every word completely resonated with me.

Hearing this song inspired me and empowered me to shine again. From her words, I drew the courage to write this book and share my message. Dark times will come in life. But you always have the choice to rise above your past and move back into your light.

Decide to shine.

1. Are you allowing your true light to shine in your life? If not, what is holding you back? What are some of your fears?

_____

_____

_____

_____

_____

_____

_____

_____

_____

2. Do you remember a time when your personal achievement exceeded your expectations? How did it make you feel? Did you feel good, or did it make you feel uncomfortable? Write it down.

_____

_____

_____

_____

_____

_____

_____

3. Create a new inner dialogue with yourself and let go of your limiting beliefs. It is time to send your ego packing. Never let other people's fears dim your own light. Allow yourself the opportunity to step into your greatness, without judgment or reservation. What goals or dreams would you go after if you knew with absolute certainty you could not fail? Pretend that you have already achieved these goals. Write them down. Imagine how it makes you feel, to allow yourself to shine?

_____

_____

_____

_____

_____

_____

_____

_____

_____

_____

_____

Chapter Twelve

Discover Your Passion

If you are interested in something, no matter what it is, go at it at full speed ahead. Embrace it with both arms, hug it, love it and above all become passionate about it. Lukewarm is no good. Hot is no good either. White hot and passionate is the only thing to be.

—Roald Dahl

Passion runs deep through my veins. It swirls inside of me like an unstoppable force, longing to be released. My soul is nourished from passion. It provides an endless supply of divine energy. With it, I become renewed and awakened to a joy that elevates me to a higher level of being. When I follow my passions, I feel an overwhelming sense of happiness.

Ever since I was a young girl, I have always been keenly aware of my passions. It is easy for me to gravitate towards things that I love and love to do. I love nature. Just the simple beauty of things stirs my soul. I am passionate about love, spending time with my family and friends, traveling, living by the coast, design, being creative, reading, learning, and yoga. One of my greatest passions that I carry in my heart is my desire to pay it forward. With absolute certainty, I know this passion is also my purpose. Inspiring others with my empowering message brings meaning to my life.

I discovered each of my passions at different points in my life. I have no doubt that, as I continue to grow and learn, I will discover new passions along the way. Sometimes you may discover a passion when you are least expecting it. A willingness to try new activities will open yourself to discovering a world of new interests.

I am sure some of you are just like me. You know exactly what sets your heart on fire and what makes you feel alive! Others of you may find being in touch with your passions a bit more challenging. Perhaps you have lost touch with your dreams and desires. Maybe you have become disconnected from the things that stir your soul. Don't worry. It is never too late to start living your life with passion.

A few years back, I ended up in this very place myself. After our business abruptly ended, my husband and I had to reassess our dreams for our future. We believed we had been following our passion with our business. However, in hindsight, this was not entirely true. We were passionate about making a difference in the lives of others. The truth was that, after it ended, a part of me was relieved. Although we put our heart and soul into its success, I was never as happy as I imagined I would be.

I came to realize that my desire to help others was overshadowing areas in my life, and I was diminishing my daily happiness. In particular, I did not enjoy making frequent trips to meet doctors at burn centers. I convinced myself early on that I could learn to come to terms with it. I overcame this hurdle and actually became very good at it. The problem was I would leave my meetings feeling completely drained and heartsick for the patients I would meet. I loved knowing we were greatly improving the lives of others with our product. But in the end, the sacrifice I was making became too great. I was leaving part of my soul behind with every burn survivor I met. I knew serving others was my purpose. But clearly, going about it in this manner was not my passion.

So the end of our business was a blessing in disguise. A sigh of relief quietly settled into my soul. Now I was free to make new dreams. At first, I was at a loss. I had no idea where to begin. It was a bit unsettling to think I had been following a dream that in the end was not my passion. I started to second-guess myself. I had always known what things brought me happiness, but somehow, this time, I got it wrong.

I knew I had to rediscover my true passions within myself. I had to quiet the part of my mind that was telling me what I should be doing. I knew my answer was buried deep beneath my thoughts. It was time to listen patiently for my soul to speak. I would only find my truth if I gave my mind a rest. In its silence, the answers I was seeking would come. In quiet meditation, I began to reconnect with my true self. What I discovered would change the course of my life forever. I did not have to sacrifice my passions in life in order to fulfill my life's purpose of healing others. This had been the critical error of my previous way of thinking. Purpose does not mean having to sacrifice passion. You could never give your absolute best if you are void of all passion. You must create a way for them to coexist.

My life began to open up in countless ways. Besides moving back to California, I began to create new dreams for myself. I never lost my desire to make a difference in the world. I now knew I had to do it in a way that I was passionate about. For me, that meant finding a way to incorporate my passion to live life beautifully with my passion to empower other women to live that way too, regardless of their circumstances.

Are you living your life with passion? Is your life a reflection of the things that make your soul soar? Are there changes you could make that would bring more passion to your daily life?

Discover your passion.

1. What makes you feel alive? Quiet your mind and allow yourself to feel the things that bring you the most joy. Write them down.

_____

_____

_____

_____

_____

_____

_____

_____

2. Do you have a clear understanding of what your passions are? What would you choose to do today if you had the freedom and the means to do it? Where would you be? Who would be around you? Write it down.

_____

_____

_____

_____

_____

_____

_____

3. If you are still disconnected from your passions, try to spend some time reconnecting with nature. Go outdoors and find a place that is relaxing and peaceful to you. Once there, free yourself from your mind's chatter and just allow yourself to be in the moment. What do you feel? Recognize any sights and sounds that appeal to you. Allow yourself to recall past memories that have made you feel alive. Start a journal, or make notes below, whenever you become aware of something that brings you (or has previously brought you) an abundance of happiness.

_____

_____

_____

_____

_____

_____

_____

Section IV

Your Fourth Piece of GOLD

Grace
Ohm: the Art of Meditation
Listen to Your Intuition
Design Your Dream Life

Chapter Thirteen

Grace

Grace is what picks me up and lifts my wings high above and I fly! Grace always conquers! Be graceful in everything; in anger, in sadness, in joy, in kindness, in unkindness, retain grace with you!
—**C. Joybell C.**

What would your life look like if you lived a life of grace? For me, living in grace means expressing love or kindness towards another—even if he may not be deserving of it. Admittedly, I have not spent my whole life living in grace, nor have I come close to mastering this modality. But my journey has provided me with a greater perspective and better understanding of the beauty that abounds when you choose to live with true grace. I have discovered that there are four pillars to living in grace: expressing compassion, showing kindness, learning to forgive, and refraining from judgment.

1. Expressing Compassion

My first lesson in grace came at an unlikely period of my life: my teenage years. Let's face it; being a teenager presents its own set of challenges. Just fitting in is a huge accomplishment in and of its self. Most teenagers are so focused on their own needs that they give little thought to the well-being of others. Grace is a foreign concept to many teens. I was no exception to this case—until after my accident.

Grace entered my life when I began to feel and express compassion. Not that I was an unfeeling person prior to this; living life as a burn survivor simply heightened my awareness of human suffering. The fire changed many things about me, but one thing it changed was the size of my heart. It grew ten times as a result of my own afflictions. I became empathetic to anyone who had to endure hardships, pain, or any type of trial. Grace was now part of my DNA.

2. Showing Kindness

I guess most people would like to think of themselves as being kind. I am certainly no different. I enjoy doing nice things for the people I love and care about; it comes easy for me. It makes me feel good to know that I am helping out a family member or friend. Isn't that what being a good person is all about?

The real challenge of grace is showing kindness to those who may not be deserving of it. Maybe you are going through a divorce, and your soon-to-be ex has been treating you badly. His actions leave you angry and hurt. Would you be willing to show him kindness if he needed your help?

What if your difficult mother in-law, whom you never could get along with, was hurting? Would you try to reach out, or turn away and pretend not to notice? Rising up and showing kindness, even when it is not merited, is living in grace.

I remember when I was going through my own divorce. It would have been easy to let anger and sadness guide my actions towards Mark. Some of my friends could not understand how I could treat him with such kindness and respect—especially when he was hurting my children and myself so badly by choosing to live apart. The truth was I *was* angry and hurt by our divorce as it was unfolding. But I was able to find compassion for him because I knew his behavior was being driven by his own hurt and suffering. It would not serve my children, Mark, or myself to be unkind or hurtful towards him. I learned that sometimes the people who are least deserving of our kindness are the ones who need it the most.

3. Learning to Forgive

Another tenet of living in grace is forgiveness. Since I devoted an entire chapter to forgiveness, I will just add a few brief points here. Learning to forgive is not without its challenges. Forgiving someone who does not deserve to be forgiven or who is without remorse is extremely difficult to do. Finding forgiveness for those who least deserve to be forgiven is living in grace.

4. Refraining from Judgment

We live in a world filled with criticism and judgments. If you turn on the TV, pick up a newspaper, or go online on any given day, you will be bombarded with negativity, gossip, and dark thoughts. The media knows that inciting fear or sensationalizing the downfall of others will draw a captive audience.

Many of our own actions are driven by our fears and insecurities. This is especially true regarding being critical or passing judgment on other people. Judgment comes from our own insecurities and self-esteem issues. It is seldom about another individual.

I remember the first time I took off my wedding ring when I was going through my divorce. On one hand, I did not want to wear it anymore because I no longer felt married. Yet I was almost paralyzed with fear at the thought of removing it. I had two small children, and now I would be announcing to the world I was a single mom. What would others think about me? Maybe they would think I was a horrible wife, a lousy mother—or maybe that I never married? A million negative thoughts flooded my mind. I recalled every judgment I previously held over other women's lives. The truth was that I knew nothing about their personal situations. My criticism of them came from my own fear and deep insecurities I had about myself. I had made my own judgments based on inaccuracies and speculation. I had no right to ever judge anyone. How could I possibly know what it was like to walk in his or her shoes?

This made me realize something else about the judgments I had been making. Not all of my wild speculations and conclusions that I made were negative. It became just as easy to make rash judgments of anyone I perceived to *have it all*. Isn't it everyone's fantasy to live a perfect life? A beautiful person living life perfectly sounds like a dream come true. But as we learned in chapter eight, there is no such thing as a perfect life. No one is immune to pain, heartache, or loss. Yet, when someone appears to have it all, we tend to feel uncomfortable and often envious. Prior to my divorce, I fell into this trap quite often. Little did I know that someone's real life circumstances could be very different than what we can see from the outside. You never gain true awareness of someone's circumstances until you walk a day in his shoes.

Live with grace.

1. Begin by showing compassion towards others who are hurting. When you open yourself to express love or compassion, you open yourself to receiving more in return.

2. Take the high road and show kindness towards an individual who may not have been especially nice to you lately. It doesn't matter how small the act of kindness is. Any kind gesture will matter. Making the choice to be kind does not mean that you should let yourself become taken advantage of. It just means that when you have the choice to act kindly, you strive to be the better person.

3. Remember that forgiveness is a gift you give yourself, even if the person you are forgiving does not deserve to be forgiven. The peace you will discover from releasing your pain comes directly from grace.

4. Think of some individuals you may have been secretly judging. There is probably much more going on in their lives than you could possibly know. Spend more time on improving your own happiness and less time scrutinizing the choices other people are making. Treat them the same way you would desire to be treated: respect them, without judgments, criticism, or negative thoughts. Thinking more positive thoughts will bring more positive results to you in your own life.

Chapter Fourteen

Ohm: The Art of Meditation

The highest goal of spirituality is Self-realization, but what does that mean? It means to feel your Self as a living reality in this moment, and there is always only this moment.
—Gay Hendricks

Today our world is filled with more distractions than ever. Our minds are constantly in motion. Negative, mindless chatter is not only a distraction, but it can hinder our ability to create ways to express ourselves to the fullest. Learning to quiet our minds, even for small increments of time, can produce many positive effects in our life.

I used to believe that people who meditated were woo-woo or earthy-crunchy. In other words, spiritually way out there. Over the past five years, my new understanding of meditation has shattered my former belief and has opened the door to a completely new way of thinking and being.

First of all, you should know that my mind is constantly going. My thoughts are often filled with new ideas. I am usually worrying, planning, preparing, remembering, creating, dreaming, analyzing—and the list goes on and on. It is not unusual for me to awaken in the middle of a deep sleep to think for hours at a time. So, you can imagine how difficult it would be for me to learn to silence my mind.

My first introduction to meditation came through yoga. I had always wanted to give it a try, but I found it a bit intimidating at first glance. An opportunity presented itself when our neighborhood club in Georgia began offering it. Karen and I decided we would take a class together. At the very least, we knew we could laugh at ourselves over our experience if it did not go exactly as well as we had hoped.

After one class, we were hooked. Although we both needed time to work on our form, we loved the time we spent doing yoga. Beyond the physical benefits, we loved the peacefulness and the mental relaxation that came with it. At the end of each class, our instructor would guide us through a simple meditation. Although it would last only a few minutes, its restorative properties lingered much longer. As much as I enjoyed doing yoga, I found myself looking forward to the meditation equally as much.

Several years later, as we were making our move back to California, we spent the summer in Maui. I was determined to make it the best summer ever.

At the top of my list of goals for the summer was learning how to meditate. Maui is one of the most peaceful and beautiful places on earth. I decided if I was ever going to give it a try, Maui was the place to do it. I had it all planned. I first would read *Eat, Pray, Love* by Elizabeth Gilbert. My spiritual journey would begin vicariously through Liz. It turns out our similarities ran deeper than our immediately apparent shared love of Italian food and adventure. We both have what she calls "monkey minds that will do anything not to be still."

I took an additional step to assure my success by purchasing some meditation downloads off of the Internet. Nothing was left to chance. However, my first attempt to meditate did not exactly go off without a hitch. Listening to my meditation tape was so relaxing that I ended up falling asleep. Perhaps playing it at bedtime, while lying comfortably in bed, was not the wisest way to start out.

The next day, I decided my likelihood of success would rise if I attempted to meditate in the morning. There was certainly less chance of falling asleep if I was refreshed and awake. With the windows wide open and the sun beaming down on my face, I played my guided meditation download and gave it another go. I concentrated on my breathing for several minutes and was feeling like I was getting the hang of it, when all of the sudden my mind began to wander. This became a reoccurring problem for me after numerous attempts to meditate. I decided I would not give up easily, so I kept practicing daily.

After several days of struggling to quiet my mind, I added a visual technique that seemed to help. I imagined my mind being tucked under the covers and into bed. I directed it to be still and stay in bed asleep. For some odd reason, this seemed to work. Like a small child who got out of bed just to test his parents' limits, my conscious mind would try to rise. Although stirring for attention, it soon settled into its new routine.

For the first time I experienced a peacefulness and full awareness of my being. Discovering how to become fully present in the moment is a wonderful gift. We spend so much of our time going from one thing to the next; we often miss the beauty that lies in a single moment. Being in Maui awakened me to becoming fully present in the moment.

After I left paradise, I had every intention of continuing my new daily practice. However, returning to all the distractions of normal, everyday activities posed more of a challenge than I would have imagined. Something had to change. I had to find a new way to incorporate meditation back into my life.

After many fits and starts, I discovered a new and easy way to meditate that is also highly effective. Its brilliance is in its simplicity. The concept is to focus on spending nine minutes each day meditating. The beauty of this technique is that you only need to do it for three minutes, three times a day.

Dina Proctor, the creator of the 3x3 meditations, came up with this revelation while trying to overcome her own challenges with being still for extended periods of time. As a result of the tremendous effects she started to see in her own life, and in the lives of those she shared it with, Dina knew she was on to something big. Dina began coaching other people on 3x3 meditations and wrote a book about her journey: *Madly Chasing Peace: How I Went from Hell to Happy in Nine Minutes a Day.* Not only is her story inspiring, her guided steps through her 3x3s are powerful. I highly recommend this book to anyone who wants to learn a simple yet highly effective way to meditate.

Now that I have adopted this new way to meditate into my daily routine, I am able to focus more on the life I want to live. Meditation helps to clear out any negative thoughts lingering in my head and replace them with empowering messages to my subconscious that are aligned with my dreams and aspirations.

Begin a meditation practice.

There are many benefits to meditating on a regular basis. Meditation helps to interrupt your mind's negative thought patterns and provides an opportunity to set new intentions and goals. Here's one way to get started.

1. First, get a timer or stopwatch and begin by setting a goal of sitting still for two or three minutes. Find a comfortable, quiet place to relax, where you know you will not be disturbed. Turn off your phone or anything else that may be a distraction. Once you are comfortable, take a few slow, deep breaths. Breathe in through your nose and then slowly release the breath through your mouth. Try focusing on your breathing, in and out. If your mind begins to wander, simply refocus on your breaths. Do this for two or three minutes, until your timer sounds off.

2. Once you begin to feel comfortable meditating for three minutes, take the next step of committing to this practice every day for a week. As you get more comfortable with it, you can build your way up to nine minutes a day.

3. If you are willing to give it a try, it will soon become part of your daily routine. Let this become sacred time you take for yourself, to give gratitude for your blessings, set new intentions for your life, and discover the answers you are seeking from the whispers of your soul.

Chapter Fifteen

Listen to
Your Intuition

We all have a better guide in ourselves, if we would attend to it,
than any other person can be.
—Jane Austen

I ntuition is one of my favorite subjects to talk about. However, it took great deliberation to decide to include it in this book. After much careful consideration, I concluded that I have an obligation to share this part of my journey with you. And of all the personal moments I have shared with you, this by far makes me feel the most vulnerable.

To be honest, for the majority of my life, the subject of intuition scared the hell out of me. Sharing my experiences now, in the context of this book, is as terrifying as it is liberating. Having once feared being psychic myself, I admit that I feared the labels and judgments I would be subjected to upon sharing my story. But most of all, I want to eliminate any fears others with similar experiences may hold. My desire is to teach you how to embrace and access the gift of intuition we all are born with.

Some of what I am about to share may sound unreal. Since I am baring all here, I will also admit that for a brief time I questioned my own sanity. But I can tell you with certainty the events I am about to share are not fiction—they are real.

Indeed, the first time I became aware of my intuitive abilities, I thought I was losing my mind. It was a Sunday in the winter of 1982. My mom had just taken my brother, sister, and me to church. We belonged to a small Lutheran church a few towns away. After church we would often stop at our local bakery and get some hard rolls for lunch. This day was no exception. As we were leaving the bakery, my mom ran into a woman from our church, and they began chatting in the parking lot. A young girl, who was just seventeen years old, had recently died. Her death was sudden and unexpected. Coming from a small town, this had many people talking. As I stood shivering in the parking lot, the strangest sensation came over me. I had this overwhelming feeling that this woman's fifteen-year-old son was going to die and that I was either going to die too or come very close to death. I knew it seemed insane, yet the feeling I was experiencing was undeniable.

I made the prudent decision not to speak a word of this to anyone. Even though I had never experienced anything like this sensation in my life, I convinced myself that it most likely was a result of hearing them discuss the young girl who had just died.

Word of her son's death, only one month later, became my living nightmare. Surely I must be crazy. How could this possibly have happened? Although he lived one town over, the news of his tragic death traveled at lightning speed. They found him with his dog's leash wrapped around his neck, and he had died. Not some random teenager or one of his brothers—it was him. Now I wasn't scared—I was terrified.

Every day, this weighed terribly on my mind. I just knew if I told a soul that I would either be locked up in a psychiatric hospital or thought of as an evil witch. There was no way I was going to risk either of those scenarios happening, so I decided to watch my back and remain silent.

For the most part, as far as the rest of my life, things were going pretty well. With the exception of this horrible secret, I was really happy. Scared but happy.

Then about six weeks later, the fire happened. As the flames began to circle my body, I remembered my intuition and knew this was it. My life was ending right before my eyes. My soul began to rise above my body. As I looked down, I saw my family sobbing over my casket. In that moment, I begged for one more chance to tell my family how much I loved them. By the grace of God, I did not die that day. An angel saved me. Maybe, for no other reason, than for me to live to share my journey with you.

After I arrived at the hospital, I was, without a doubt, in shock. As shocking as it was to have such a close brush with death, I was freaking out more than ever that I had some prior knowledge of these tragic events weeks before they occurred. Within a few days of being in the hospital, I had my mother call our pastor. I needed some religious counseling fast. Having watched my share of horror movies previous to this, I believed that if I was possessed, I wanted him to free me of any evil spirits that were haunting me.

Pastor Tom came quickly and tried his best to comfort me. Unfortunately, he had few answers for the many questions I had, especially in regards to the hanging death of the poor boy who had gone to our church. He gave me communion and prayed for my healing and recovery. I was left with my truth, but no answers.

After some time, I came to realize that I might never understand how I came to know what I knew. I had little choice but to accept it while holding on to the truth. I reflected more heavily on my past, trying to recall if I ever had any previous premonitions.

It didn't take long for me to recognize that this was not the first time this had happened to me. It certainly hadn't been as alarming or unsettling as my vision before my accident, but I realized that I had been having premonitions since I was three.

I can still remember the first time it happened with absolute clarity. My dad and mom were taking my brother Michael and I to our grandparents' house when I was three years old. My mom was in labor, so they were going to take care of us for the time being. As we were driving past a restaurant, about a mile from their home, I had a vision. I had no idea what it meant at the time, but I can remember it today, with precise detail. I saw the baby my mom was going to have. Although no one knew the sex of the baby at that moment, I knew I was going to have a sister. It was as though I was looking up at her. She was looking down at me. The craziest part about it was that I did not see her as a baby. She was a grown woman I had never seen before. I just knew she was my sister. I saw her face perfectly, and most memorable was her hair. It was very different than mine. Her hair was luscious. It was golden blonde, with ringlets of curls. My hair was platinum blonde, very thin, and straight as a board. The woman I saw was beautiful. I never saw or knew anyone like her before, but somehow I just knew she was my sister. My heart filled with such gratitude that I was getting a sister. Nothing could have made me happier. If you could see Susie today, you would know that she is, without a doubt, the beautiful woman I saw before my mom gave birth.

When I remembered this event, it became easier to recall other similar occurrences. This feeling of *knowing* does not come from my mind. When it occurs, it is not a thought. It comes from deep within my soul. The knowledge resonates within me on a cellular level. Though I may go for extended periods of time without experiencing it at all, when it arrives, I gladly welcome it.

It was several years after my accident before I had another premonition. One of the most unusual things about my premonitions was that often the information I would know had nothing to do with me at all. It was usually about someone I had never met before. Oddly enough, it was frequently regarding someone famous.

Growing up, one of my favorite shows to watch was *The Price Is Right*. Whenever I was home from school during the day, I would tune in. One day I will never forget was in the fall of 1985. It was a Friday, and for some reason, I was home from school that day. I remember on that particular day, after watching *The Price Is Right*, I had this sinking feeling come over me. It was about Johnny Olson, the lovable announcer on the show. Something bad was about to happen to him. It was the same feeling I had come to recognize. The following Monday, it was announced that Johnny Olson had unexpectedly passed away. I was baffled at how I could have sensed such a thing about someone I never had met.

Shortly after this, I had another vision. I was going into New York City to have dinner with my family. While we were on our way, I had this feeling that I was going to see Rob Lowe and Melissa Gilbert, who were dating at the time. I had no reason to think I would see either of them. Before we headed to the restaurant, we decided to do some shopping. Who ended up standing next to me, while looking at scarves in Bergdorf Goodman? I am sure you can guess by now that it was Melissa Gilbert.

I had small, seemingly insignificant premonitions for years to follow. I was frustrated I could never understand how to make them come more frequently. But just before my marriage blew apart, I had a premonition that was so strong and frightening that it reminded me of the one I had before my accident. I decided I was going to confide in my sister. I knew she was the only one I could trust, who would not judge my sanity. Maybe this time, if I shared my premonition, this terrible event would never happen.

I told her that I had the same feeling I had before my accident. I knew something terrible was about to happen to me. It was going to feel like a death, but it wouldn't be an actual death. Nonetheless, I knew it was about to rip my world apart. She tried her best to calm my fears. She attributed my fears to being scared of the immense happiness I was feeling. I prayed Suz was right, but I could not ignore what I was sensing deep in my soul. Even though I never anticipated my marriage exploding the way it did, I was not completely shocked. It was, indeed, the death-like event that turned my world upside down.

I also noticed that I was becoming much more in tune with my intuition. The more that I became aware of it, and less fearful of it, the more that I began to see it unfold. It was as though it had been bottled up for years, and once released, just kept flowing. One of the best things that happened to me as a result of listening to my intuition was the birth of Martha Love. Now you'll see why I needed to wait until now to share the full story. Even as I write this, the events that unfolded that day still seem wild and utterly surreal. Here is the backstory that led up to that fateful day.

In 1998, my sister thought it would be fun for us to have a girl's day in New York City with my mom and sister-in-law Tracy. Susie got us tickets to see Barbara Walters' new talk show, *The View*. She thought it would be a fun distraction from the gloom of my impending divorce, which was becoming all-consuming. The day the tickets arrived in the mail, I knew it would be life changing. I told Susie that I could not shake the feeling that somehow this show was going to help us with our careers. I had no idea how; I just knew. I was not going to leave anything to chance. I desperately tried to come up with a creative explanation, but to no avail. Nothing came to me. Yet, I was sure it would be a golden opportunity I did not want to miss.

The day of the show came, and I woke up extremely frustrated. I couldn't help feeling I missed a great opportunity. We spent the night at my parents' home in New Jersey. As we were getting ready to leave, my sister came down dressed in an awful white suit. It looked like she robbed it from Mr. Roarke's wardrobe, from *Fantasy Island*. (Although *Fantasy Island* was another favorite childhood television show of mine, there was nothing stylish about this look.) There was no way I could let her leave the house looking like this, especially since she was also born with a sense of style. I suggested she quickly throw on one of the cute sundresses she made while living in Maui.

While I was driving in to the city, I kept having the same reoccurring message play over and over in my head: "If someone asks Susie about her dress, tell them she designed it." It kept repeating like a broken record. After we finally arrived at the studio, settling into the back of the line, we were approached by some producers of the show. They asked us if we would be interested in staying for another show and being part of a segment hula hooping with Richard Simmons and some *Cosmopolitan* bachelors. The other girls were on board, so I agreed it would be fun. After the first show taped, they had everyone in the audience leave but the four of us. They brought us down to practice with some of the guys who had been named as *Cosmopolitan* magazine's bachelors of the year. Yes, the bachelors were hot! What made it even more fun was having some of the guys from the soap opera *All My Children* come and check out what we were doing. It turned out that the cast of *All My Children* taped their show in a studio next door. It was turning into a fun day after all. Little did I know it would only get better.

We were given front-row seats for the taping of the next show. During the first commercial break, a co-host from *The View* came up to my sister and told her she loved her dress. Without hesitation, I blurted out that she designed it. Before we knew it, Susie was invited backstage to meet with her. One of the co-hosts of this wildly popular show wanted Susie to make her a dress. That was the moment I had been waiting for. I was completely dialed into my intuition. I just knew that coming to this show was going to be an opportunity to help us with our careers. I never imagined it would be as fashion designers. I learned to listen to my intuition, and it paid off. We ran with this new opportunity and began our new business overnight.

Many fun and unique opportunities came as a result of our new careers. Within the year, we suddenly found ourselves being asked to do trunk shows for boutiques and department stores. Initially, I didn't even know what a trunk show was. A trunk show is an invitation for a designer to share her line as a featured guest in stores. It was exciting and humbling to be asked, so we jumped at our first opportunity.

We were invited to do a trunk show for a very chic, upscale boutique on Nantucket. My sister and I had an extra-special place in our hearts for Nantucket, as our grandparents and dad spent many summers vacationing there. Granddaddy, an art director, was passionate about painting watercolor landscapes of Nantucket, and our family was blessed to be the beneficiary of his passion. Naturally, we were so excited to do a trunk show there.

We decided we were going to make the most of the weekend, so we invited my mom and Aunt Dee along to enjoy it with us. We arrived filled with excitement and the desire to make it an unforgettable weekend. Never in our wildest dreams did we ever expect the events that unfolded.

We arrived on Thursday evening. We were being showcased as featured designers for the following two days. We quickly had to get ready to go the next day. We managed to grab a quick bite and enjoy some time that evening. The island was abuzz with the big wedding taking place that weekend. Everyone was talking about the former cast members of *Beverly Hills, 90210*, who were reportedly going to be guests at the wedding. Susie and I joked that maybe we would get to meet one of them if they came into the boutique. After all, it was a small island.

The first day went really well. We had a great response to our line of dresses. We couldn't have hoped for more. The next day, as we were getting dressed to spend the day at the boutique, I had this funny feeling come over me. I was starting to know this feeling intimately by now. I trusted my feeling; it was just that the information I was receiving seemed illogical and crazy. I decided if there was any one in the world I could share it with, it was my sister—no matter how insane it sounded.

I said, "Suz, you know I seldom get this feeling, but when I do, I can't ignore it. Well, as crazy as it may sound, I need to share it with you. If I don't share it now, no one will ever believe me after the fact. So, here it is: I have this vision that today we are going to meet Kevin Costner and his daughter, and they are going to buy one of our dresses. I know how absolutely ridiculous it sounds, but I had to say it and just put it out there."

She just kind of smiled and most likely thought to herself, *Yeah, that* is *out there.*

Regrettably, the day began with news of a tragedy. Soon it was all over the news that the plane carrying John Kennedy Jr., his wife Carolyn, and her sister went missing the night before. It was on route to Martha's Vineyard. I felt sick hearing the news. I would have felt terrible hearing it about anyone, but especially about John Kennedy and his family. A year earlier, I was in New York City in a last-ditch effort to save my marriage. After a failed attempt to meet with Mark, I left with tears in my eyes. As I was heading back to Grand Central Station, I looked up and saw John Kennedy. I would have recognized him anywhere. He was so handsome. Even more than his undeniable good looks, I loved that he seemed to be a really down-to-earth, good guy. In this brief moment, when I saw him, our eyes met, and we exchanged smiles. I will never know if his smile was in exchange for the one I gave him, or a kind gesture to a woman whose pain was clearly written all over her face. Either way, I will always remember how his kindness made me feel.

I was heartsick to learn of his passing. The whole island was. It was difficult to keep my mind focused on anything else. That is, until my sister said to me, "Kate, turn around. Kevin Costner just came into the store with one of his daughters." I felt the blood rushing from my head. I thought for sure I was going to pass out. Not because a celebrity came in, but because it was exactly as I saw it in my premonition. It may have been one of the happiest moments of my life. Not because he told us how lovely we looked, or that he bought one of our dresses for his daughter (both of which actually did happen). My absolute joy came from knowing I finally had 100 percent, undeniable proof that I was not CRAZY! I was incredibly grateful I had confided in my sister. Once and for all, it was time for me to stop questioning my own sanity.

It was definitely a turning point in my life. I could finally put to rest any notion that my gifts were in some way dangerous, shameful, or figments of my imagination. My psychic ability is a gift. Although I may be more gifted than some, I believe everyone is born with some level of intuition. It just comes easier for some than it does for others. I once heard it compared to singing. With few exceptions, just about everyone has the ability to sing. Some people sing so well they go on to become performers. Then there are some like me, who *can* sing, but anyone with ears (particularly men, women, children, babies, and even dogs) would greatly appreciate it if I do not. Even though I have the physical ability to sing, and hard work and training may improve my natural ability, I will never be as good as those who are gifted in singing.

Getting in touch with your intuition takes practice, patience, and some perseverance. It takes time to learn how to distinguish true intuition from desires or fears created in your mind. And, like singing, it is possible to learn how to develop your intuitive abilities. I have worked with some respected teachers who have helped me further to understand and enhance my abilities through meditation, Reiki, and other tools.

The most important message I want to convey regarding intuition is that you are intuitive too. Please do not fear this ability, but choose to embrace it. Let go of any negative assumptions or stigmas you may have about your intuitive abilities or your sixth sense. Your intuition will provide the best advice you will ever hear—once you learn how to recognize its voice. If you are willing to invest a little time, you will become more aware of your inner wisdom too!

Tap into your intuition.

1. If you are unsure of your intuitive abilities, relax. It is never too late to begin working on them. Now might be a good time to take a few minutes and recall any instances when you had a feeling about or knew something before it actually happened. Maybe the phone rang, and you were just thinking about that person; or you took an umbrella to work even though there was no chance of rain, and it rained anyway. No matter how insignificant the event may have seemed at the time, it may be your intuition at work. Write down any events or incidents that come to mind.

_____

_____

_____

_____

_____

_____

2. Try meditation. Meditation helps to clear and quiet your mind so you can start your journey toward becoming more intuitive. A quiet mind is more likely to hear the whispers of your intuitive voice. If you struggle to meditate, try spending more time outdoors. Focus on the stillness and the sounds of nature. Become more aware of the sights, sounds, and smells around you. The more often you spend time in quiet, the easier it will become to connect with your intuition.

3. Keep a journal. Write down any situation where you felt you were guided with knowledge. Did it come in the form of a dream, a vision, a feeling of knowing, or something you just sensed in your being? How does this knowledge seem different than just a regular dream or thought? Write down every time you had a gut feeling, and it turned out to be correct. The more you become aware of your abilities, the easier it will be to develop them.

   Note: Although each and every one of you has intuition and, therefore, some level of psychic abilities, it does *not* mean that everyone has the ability to become a trusted psychic and provide guidance or insight for the future.

   Yes, there are certainly many respected and trusted psychics and mediums out there. However, if you desire to seek guidance from one, I strongly urge you to do your homework. Do not assume every advertised psychic will be an honest guide. Do your research and make sure to get strong referrals from individuals you trust.

Chapter Sixteen

Visualize having what you already want, feeling the feelings of already having it. Come out of that and focus on what you're grateful for already, and really enjoy it. Then go into your day and release it to the Universe and trust that the Universe will figure out how to manifest it.

—Jack Canfield

Many people recognize they are not happy or content with their current circumstances. Yet often they do not have a vision or clear plan about how to create the things they desire in their lives. Are you unhappy or unfulfilled in your life, but unsure if it is even possible to change your circumstances? Are feelings of being trapped or frozen with fear holding you back from living a life you desire? The good news is that it is never too late to make positive changes and design your dream life.

I fell into the same trap countless times in my own life. I believed I was stuck in my circumstances and had to give up on my dreams. Certainly, for a long period after the fire, I had given up that I would ever achieve my dream of finding a deep, passionate, loving relationship with a man who loved me back the same way. After some time, I was able to allow myself to dream that it just might be possible. I remember creating the following image in my mind: I visualized myself falling in love with a handsome, strong, intelligent man. He was caring and compassionate. We shared similar dreams and aspirations for a life of adventure. We were not only very much in love, but we were also best friends. One day we would marry and create a family of our own. I pictured us living in a beautiful home. We were extremely blessed and enjoyed life to the fullest. This was the dream I held in my heart and saw vividly in my mind. It seemed completely out of reach, but that did not keep me from dreaming about it. I wanted it more than I ever wanted anything in my life.

Looking back, it sometimes still amazes me that it did not remain my dream. It became my life. Two of the biggest reasons I believe I was able to make my dreams a reality are (1) I created a picture of my dream life in my heart, and (2) I took action.

Do you know exactly what you want in your life? Do you have a clear image of the people you desire around you, your ideal place to live, and what you could do that would bring you the most joy and happiness? Maybe you have disconnected yourself from your dreams because you gave up on ever receiving them, or you've lost touch with what you want in your life right now. The great news is that you can begin today to ignite the fire of your passions and unleash the dreams of your soul.

If you are like some and do not know where to begin, start with a dream board. I can't remember the first time I ever made a dream board, but it was probably at least fifteen years ago. A dream board is a collage or poster with photos and phrases that create a picture of what your dream life would look like for you. You simply cut out and paste on it a representation of anything you wish to manifest in your life. Your only limit is your imagination or desires. Put pictures of anything that resonates with you, instilling feelings of happiness, peace, and abundance. The most important element of your board is that it should represent the life you want for yourself. Let go of fear, judgment, or limiting beliefs. Let yourself be free to create from your deepest desires.

By creating your vision board, you begin to take the first steps of bringing your dreams to life. Every time you look at your board, focus intently. Imagine that you have already created this life for yourself. Allow yourself to feel how wonderful this life is and release positive emotions. Each time you do this, you raise your vibrational level and send a strong message to your subconscious. You and everything around you is made of energy. Negative energy vibrates at very low frequency levels. Positive energy vibrates at a much higher frequency. Negative energy attracts more negative energy. The same is true for positive energy. The more positive energy you create, the more positive energy you attract. Every time you have a negative thought enter your mind, try replacing it with a positive thought or positive affirmation. The more frequently you do this, the more positive results you will begin to see in your life.

If you want to take this a step further, create a mind movie. I first heard of this concept from Natalie Ledwell, one of the co-creators of Mind Movies. It is a super cool tool that will add another dimension to your dream board. The idea is that creating a movie on your computer of your personal photos, life affirmations, and favorite music can bring your vision to a whole new level in order more powerfully to manifest your dreams and desires. Being a visual person myself, I absolutely love this idea. What could be better than hearing your favorite songs as the soundtrack to the movie of your ideal life? Not only has the mind movie been a wonderful aid to lift my spirits, I have been blown away by how many of my dreams have already begun to manifest. My husband even made a mind movie of his own. We had fun sharing some of the same images and aspirations we both desire.

Rhonda Byrnes gives many powerful examples of using visualization and dream boards in her book, *The Secret*. John Assaraf, a contributor to *The Secret*, gives one of the most extraordinary. Having created dream boards for many years, he was blown away to realize he was living in the actual house he had cut out and added to his dream board years earlier. He has gone on to do extensive research and has become a leading expert on the power of the brain, teaching others how to create their dream lives too.

Another powerful tool for creating the life you want is to write down your dreams and desires on paper. When you write anything down, you are making an imprint in your mind. The more you reread your affirmation and put positive energy behind it, the more it will become real to your subconscious. When you write out your affirmations, make sure they are in the present tense. Some examples of the affirmations I write are, as follows: "I am happier than I have ever been. I am so blessed to be part of a loving family, living in a beautiful ocean-view home. I love inspiring and empowering people around the world to live their most beautiful life. I am so grateful for all of the blessings in my life." The more descriptive you can be, the more real your affirmations will become to you.

Jack Canfield and Mark Victor Hansen, authors of the *Chicken Soup for the Soul* series, have become masters at using this technique themselves. Before, during, and after the release of their first *Chicken Soup for the Soul* book, they wrote down their dreams and wishes for the success of their book on sticky notes and posted them on everything they could. Today, the series, which has over 250 titles, has sold more than 110 million copies in 54 languages around the world. They firmly believe that their vision, positive mindset, and written affirmations directly contributed to their enormous success.

Design your dream life.

1. What does your dream life look like? Where do you live? Who are you with? What are you doing that lights up your life? Let go of any limiting beliefs. Write your vision down, and describe it in detail. Be as specific as possible.

_____

_____

_____

_____

_____

_____

_____

_____

_____

_____

2. Make your own dream board or mind movie. Cut out pictures from magazines or go online and search for pictures of anything you want to create in your own life. Pinterest is an excellent place to start. (You are welcome to follow my board. Go to www.beautyunfoldingbook.com, to be connected.) You can even make your own board online. After you are finished making a dream board or mind movie, make sure you keep it

somewhere you can see it often. Take some time to look at it daily. Start to imagine that this is your life today.

3. Write out your dream life as affirmations. Describe your perfect life in detail. Make a habit of writing it out and reading it daily— several times a day, if possible. Writing along with reading your affirmations is extremely powerful because it will help to create a stronger imprint in your mind, as well as your subconscious. Post copies of your affirmations on your desk, bathroom mirror, or any other place it will be highly visible.

Section V

Your Fifth Piece of GOLD

Generosity
Opportunity Is Everywhere
Live Beautifully
Decisive Action

Chapter Seventeen

Generosity

Some people give time, some money, some their skills or connections, some literally give their life's blood. But everyone has something to give.
—**Barbara Bush** (American First Lady, 1989–1993)

E veryone is blessed with talents and gifts. Our gifts blossom the most when we freely share them with others. When you give with the sole purpose to help another, you open yourself to countless blessings in return. One of the best feelings in the world is knowing you are helping to make a difference in someone else's life.

Just as everyone is blessed with talents and gifts, everyone can give. Giving does not require money or any special qualifications. It doesn't have to be a grand act. You only need to have a desire to give and the follow through to take action. Every thoughtful deed does matter. Even the smallest acts of kindness can make a huge difference in another person's life. Even the simplest acts of kindness have the potential to cause a ripple effect of goodwill throughout the Universe.

If you are at a low point in your life and feel as though you have nothing to give, you may be surprised to know that now more than ever is the time to give back. Ironically, your generosity can have the greatest impact during the times you feel you have nothing to give—not only for others, but for you as well.

I know firsthand how a simple act of kindness has the power to transform someone's life. The nameless stranger who came to visit me during one of my darkest hours in the hospital only spent a matter of minutes with me. Little did she know that she was giving me the most precious gift I could ever have received. She gave me back my life. After that day, I never saw her again. I deeply regret never having the chance to thank her for what she did for me. To be honest, I never even asked her what her name was. This bothered me terribly for years. I finally realized that, to me, her name could only be *Hope*. Although I had no way to thank her properly for saving my life, I would honor her gift by paying it forward.

I have tried to live my life always being mindful of Hope's kindness. When Chelsea and Carter were still very young, Mark and I began to pay her gift forward with trips to visit the children in hospitals during the holidays. We brought gifts to try to cheer them up and spent some time visiting with them as well. It certainly tore at our heartstrings, but we hoped that somehow we were making a difference.

A few years ago, when we were in Maui while making our way back to California, as a family we decided to volunteer with Hale Kau Kau. We learned about Hale Kau Kau (which is Hawaiian for House of Meals) from my parents. My parents regularly volunteer on Maui to deliver meals to homebound individuals through this organization. Since my parents were off-island at the time, we thought it would be a great opportunity to get our family involved. We decided to take over my parents' route for the summer.

Our family had been through a lot over the past several years, and without a doubt, it had taken its toll on our family. In addition to the devastating losses and heartbreak we endured, during the four years leading up to that summer, four out of our five family members had had serious health issues. However, we felt very fortunate that none of them were life threatening. We knew we had much to be grateful for, so we wanted to help those who were not as fortunate. Hale Kau Kau was a perfect fit.

We were only needed one day a week. It usually only took about an hour and a half to two hours of our time, which always flew by quickly. It brought each of us such joy to know we were helping others. Since all of the meals were going to homebound seniors, they were especially appreciative of the time we spent talking with them. They loved getting to know our children and often said it was the best part of their week. Their smiles and appreciation lifted our spirits more than we could have imagined. It was such an honor for us to get to know each of them. It was impossible to distinguish the joy we were bringing to each of these wonderful individuals from the joy we were actually receiving ourselves.

There are scores of ways to give of yourself to others. The easiest way to start is to find something you already enjoy doing and find a way to help someone else with your gift. Maybe you love to cook. Try making a meal for someone. Numerous times I have had a friend or neighbor go through a difficult time, and instead of feeling helpless, I offer to bring a meal or to lend a hand around their home. I have even picked up groceries and helped with chores. If someone is not well or is facing adversity, the smallest acts of kindness are often appreciated the most.

Here are some other ways you could make a difference in someone else's life:

- Offer to help out at your child's school.
- Donate food or clothing or household items to a food bank or shelter.
- Knit a beanie or a blanket for newborns in the hospital.
- Donate your hair to www.locksoflove.org.
- Walk, run, or bike for a charity (see www.avonwalk.org, www.the3day.org, or www.charitymiles.org).
- Visit or spend time with someone who is homebound.
- Adopt a homeless pet from a shelter (www.petfinder.com).
- Ask that, in lieu of a gift for your birthday or other special occasion, friends or family make a donation to a favorite charity. Some of my personal favorites are, as follows:
  - St. Jude Children's Research Hospital: www.stjude.org
  - Phoenix Society: www.phoenix-society.org
  - Angelwish: www.angelwish.org
  - Heifer International: www.heifer.org
  - American Red Cross: www.redcross.org
  - Feed the Children: www.feedthechildren.org

If you are ready to take a bolder step and make a long-term commitment, volunteering is a great way to serve others. You can find endless opportunities to volunteer in your community, or if you are really adventurous, you can travel to faraway places. Whether you want to make a difference in the life of a child, another adult, or in the world around you, think about volunteering for one of these great charities:

- Habitat for Humanity: www.habitat.org
- Be the Match Registry: www.bethematch.org

- Girls Inc.: www.girlsinc.org
- Big Brother Big Sister of America: www.bbbs.org
- Best Buddies International: www.bestbuddies.org
- Special Olympics: www.specialolympics.org
- Wounded Warriors: www.woundedwarriorproject.org
- Surfrider Foundation: www.surfrider.org

For the most dedicated and determined individuals who want to make a difference, you can start your own charity. Individuals who have suffered great hardship or loss themselves start some of the best charities. Starting a charity can be one of the most healing and rewarding ways to rise above adversity. It is also an incredible way to honor the memory of a friend or loved one who has passed on.

Make a difference.

1. If you are hesitant or nervous about giving back, start small. Begin with small acts of kindness that do not require a big time commitment and are not out of your comfort zone. Try doing something that comes easy to you and share it with others. Maybe you could lend your voice or gardening skills to your church or synagogue, make a meal for a friend in need, or donate some clothing or goods to a charity, such as Baby Buggy (www.babybuggy.org) or Dress for Success (www.dressforsuccess.org).

2. Think about some charities or organizations that are meaningful to you. Ask friends or family to make a donation in your name on your next birthday or special occasion.

3. Just do it! Even if you are still struggling to recognize the gifts you can offer someone else, know you can make a difference in the lives of others. You have talents and gifts to share with the world. You will only discover how magnificent these gifts really are when you freely give them to others. Write down three things you could do that would help someone else out or brighten her day.

_____

_____

_____

_____

_____

_____

_____

_____

_____

_____

_____

_____

_____

Chapter Eighteen

Opportunity Is Everywhere

Each problem has hidden in it an opportunity so powerful that it literally dwarfs the problem. The greatest success stories were created by people who recognized a problem and turned it into an opportunity.

—Joseph Sugarman

When one door closes, another one opens. This saying has always been true. But today, we are so fortunate to live in a world where more opportunities seem to exist than any other time in history. Too often opportunities are missed because we spend our time focusing on misfortune rather than the positive possibilities accompanying it.

If you are unhappy with your life, or do not like the changes that are happening, do not despair. An abundance of opportunity is available to you in your situation, waiting for you to grab hold of it. But you can only see these possibilities when you shift to a positive mindset and expand your range of thinking. Some of the best opportunities come in a different package than you might have expected and too often end up becoming *lost* or *missed* opportunities.

I have experienced both sides of this coin myself, having both seized and missed opportunities. Recognizing our opportunity to start a career in fashion design during our day at *The View* only happened because my sister and I were open to possibility. If we hadn't already made that positive mindset shift, our day at *The View* would have ended up only being a fun memory, with the bonus of my sister receiving a nice compliment on her dress.

Although I have few regrets in my life, I do deeply regret letting one incredible opportunity slip away. In 1999, while I was living in Westport, Connecticut, I was blessed to meet Karen Fernandez. I was introduced to her through a mutual friend. She and I soon became friends, and she graciously offered to help me build my business. Karen worked tirelessly with me to grow my line of handbags. I will be forever grateful for having Karen in my life.

Soon after my bags had launched, ABC News ran a story on Martha Love. To my amazement, our phones were ringing off the hook. Dozens and dozens of opportunities were flooding in. I was completely unprepared and overwhelmed by the response to the story. Karen came to my rescue and was fielding all of my calls for me. At the time, I was at a loss for words. I was not prepared for the amazing opportunities that were unleashed.

One of the calls Karen received was from a company who wanted to speak to me about doing a licensing agreement to make Martha Love shoes. They were very high end and represented an extremely impressive list of designers. *Believing* I was not prepared to even speak with them at the time, I asked if I could call them back. I ended up losing this golden opportunity, because they lost interest after postponing our discussion. It was a very bitter pill to swallow and became one of my biggest single regrets. However, the lesson I learned that day will stick with me forever. If you are presented with a great opportunity, seize it. Do not walk away from something because of a fear of failure.

One of the key elements to spotting opportunities is rethinking what you define as *negative* in your life. No one likes to see the end of something she desired to have in her life. Have faith that good things can come out of seemingly negative situations. Every obstacle, challenge, or loss will bring new opportunities your way. You will be amazed at the endless possibilities that will arise when you embrace a positive mindset.

Open the door to opportunity.

1. Start looking for the open doors! Do not allow yourself to become paralyzed with fear or negativity because one door has closed. Embrace change.

2. Take some time to reassess your life. What do you love and want more of? What is it that you don't like or that is missing in your life? Once you discover what truly matters to you in your life, begin to think of ways to become closer to your goals.

3. Think of your life as a great book. You have just finished an incredible chapter in your life. Now you can hardly wait to see what lies in store for you next! Grab a pen. Become the heroine/ hero in your life, and do not settle for being a victim. Your life is ultimately your story to write. Remember, you always

have creative control over your thoughts and choices. What new adventures are in store for you in your next chapter?

Chapter Nineteen

Live Beautifully

Life is beautiful . . . so choose to live beautifully.
—**Kate Waite**

I have always been passionate about living beautifully. My desire to live fully and embrace all of the beauty life holds is still true for me today. Although it was a struggle at times, I have come to learn the meaning of true beauty. From my desire, insight, and some creativity, I have found simple and inexpensive ways to live a beautiful life. I'd like to share with you a few easy, actionable tips to help you recognize how you can begin to live beautifully too, regardless of your current circumstances.

We live in a world that often places too much emphasis on physical beauty. Real beauty has nothing to do with your physical appearance.

Real beauty can't be bought. Yet it is accessible to anyone. Living beautifully and radiating true beauty can only come when you allow your own light to shine brilliantly. When your soul is illuminated by divine light, it is free of judgments, criticisms, and negativity. You are then able to see clearly the beauty in yourself and the world around you. The most beautiful people in the world are the ones who radiate beauty from within. Living beautifully blooms from the inside out.

Living beautifully means loving yourself just as you are. You can start living beautifully when you learn to let go of self-judgment and criticism. I know firsthand how challenging this may seem to some of you. The good news is that even in the most trying of circumstances, it is possible to rise above them. Learning to accept my new body and the reality that I would always have severe physical scars was no easy feat, especially as a teenage girl. I had to learn to love the skin I was in.

Of course, accepting my scars was very different than finding a way to love them. It was not until very recently that I began to see my scars in a completely new light.

Recently, I was relaxing on the beach, alone. I was wearing what had become my usual beach attire since my accident: a one-piece swimsuit with a sarong tied at my waist, hanging just below my left knee. Sometimes I will wear a bikini top and bottom, but I would never go without my skirt. Over the years, my beach cover-up has been my security blanket. I would never have dreamed of going to the beach or near a pool without it. On this particular day, I saw a woman walk by with several tattoos that covered a large portion of her body. Personally, I have never had any desire to get a tattoo. However, I recognize that they represent artistic expression. Tattoos often reflect a significant or meaningful snippet in someone's life. Seeing this woman led me to ask myself, "Is there beauty in our scars?"

For the first time in my life, I began to wonder if I could ever find beauty in my burns. I decided to take some photos of my scars to see if they held some hidden beauty I had been missing. After taking some photos, I wanted to see what would happen if I added warmer or cooler tones to my pictures. The results were shocking. For the first time since my accident, I was able to see the beauty that had escaped me all these years. It was now right in front of me. They were the same weathered burns. The only difference was that I was able to look at them through a different lens and gain a whole new perspective on what I was seeing. It took my breath away. (If you would like to see these photos of my scars, go to http://www.beautyunfoldingbook.com.)

This experience redefined the way I view beauty. I now am able to see something beautiful in all of my scars—emotional or physical. Over the years, I have come to witness the beauty unfolding from my emotional scars. Yet I struggled to ever find anything beautiful in the physical scars I carried. This new understanding was a huge turning point in my life. My scars paint a picture of a moment that was incredibly significant in my life. It is said that often artists create their most beautiful work from a place of pain and struggle. So too, this beautiful work of art emerged from my most tragic and painful circumstances. Like any piece of art, those who are willing to shift their perspective can see its beauty. However, its beauty will go unrecognized by those unwilling to take a closer look. My wish is that you too may open yourself to the possibility that deep beneath your scars, *emotional or physical*, there is some beauty, which is waiting to unfold.

Allowing yourself to be genuine is another way to allow beauty into your life. Let others see the real you. You deny the brilliance of your true beauty when you try to hide your authenticity from others. When you hold on to feelings of shame or low self-esteem, you live in a place of darkness. Darkness only casts a shadow over beauty. Your beauty shines most brilliantly when you are able to love yourself unconditionally, just as you are.

Take pride in yourself. Be the best version of *you* that you can be. Lovingly care for yourself. Knowing that you will start each day putting your best foot forward gives you a sense of pride. Treat yourself with respect. When you respect yourself, you send a strong message out into the world that others should respect you too.

Think about the way you see the world and how you treat others. A smile filled with warmth and love has the power to shine as brightly as the sun. When you become centered in your highest self, you rise above negative influences. Positive energy and loving thoughts come from a divine light, which, when refracted from within your soul, radiates beauty.

Observe the beauty around you. It is a gift often taken for granted. Living beautifully can only happen when you become aware of the beauty that already exists within your life. Allow all of your senses to experience nature. Immerse yourself in the sights, sounds, and smells that surround you in your favorite places.

Get organized. Being organized creates a beautiful environment and clears the clutter from your life. It is another way to tell the world that you respect yourself. Creating a neat and organized environment will bring peace and contentment to your life. It will also remove the unnecessary stress that comes with living in disarray.

Create an environment that is beautiful. It does not matter how much you have; it is what you make of it that counts. Simple, inexpensive touches can brighten any space. A fresh coat of paint is one inexpensive way to brighten up a room. Another is to add some decorative pieces that you love. Accessorize your living space with only the things that make you feel really good to have around. Some of my favorite pieces in our home I have picked up while traveling. Whether it is a beautiful piece of coral, sea sponges, or shells that I collected on a beach, or some inexpensive pots I uncovered in a small shop in Paris, everything I display has meaning to me. It is not about having *stuff*. Living beautifully is about surrounding yourself with the simple pleasures that bring you joy.

Start living beautifully today.

1. Embrace your own beauty. Let go of any fears or insecurities you may have about yourself. Celebrate your uniqueness, and let it shine! Remember, *real* beauty radiates from the inside out.

2. Become more aware of the beauty that already exists around you. Make note of anything you can do to add more simple pleasures into your daily life. (Cut some flowers or branches from outdoors to bring some added cheer into your home. Make an inexpensive meal to share with someone you enjoy being around. Get in the car to drive, or take a walk, to someplace that makes you feel good.)

3. Living beautifully is a mindset. Anyone who wishes to live more beautifully can do it. Surround yourself with the people and things that bring you joy. Do not let yourself be limited by your imagination. Living beautifully does not require wealth. It is about creating and living an authentic life and enjoying it to the fullest.

Chapter Twenty

Decisive Action

I know that I have the ability to achieve the object of my Definite Purpose in life, therefore, I demand of myself persistent, continuous action toward its attainment, and I here and now promise to render such action.

—Napoleon Hill

The best ideas and plans will never come to fruition if you do not take action. Dreams will remain dreams unless a strategic plan is made and action is taken. You have been given the foundation and the tools to create a beautiful life for yourself. Now is the time to take action!

Dreaming of a beautiful life and taking action to create one are two very different things. Dreaming, admittedly, is much each easier. It requires only your imagination and no effort on your part at all. Taking action, without a doubt, requires effort on your part. Action will be the only way to reap happiness and rewards.

Once you have decided what you wish to create in your life, you need to devise a plan. The bigger the dream, the more thought you need to put in your plan. It is great to dream big. Do not let the size or scope of your desires discourage you from going after them. You may need to set realistic expectations and a realistic timeframe for them to evolve.

Taking action is usually the "make it or break it" point. Actually making a plan and then taking action requires you to be bold, have faith, and be willing to take some risk. There are few guarantees in life—except that if you keep doing the same thing, you will most likely get the same results. If you have a strong desire to get more out of your life, you must be willing to push yourself out of your comfort zone. You have to want it passionately and be willing to make some sacrifices to have it. Do not let fear stand in your way. You must desire this change so much that you are willing to go for it—even in the face of uncertainty and fear. Change can sometimes feel scary. It is often the very thing that stops most people dead in their tracks as they pursue their dreams.

I had to face my own fears about becoming an author. I had always wanted to write a book. I knew I had a message to share with others, yet I completely doubted my ability actually to write about it. I was always waiting for the perfect moment or proverbial lightning bolt from the sky that would confirm beyond a doubt that I could turn my dream into reality. Shockingly enough, it never happened. The truth was that I had to decide that I was going to go after my big, bodacious dream—in spite of my fears and insecurities and lack of guarantees. I had to come to a place where I was no longer willing to settle. I loved so much about my life, but I dreamed of more.

My husband and I were no strangers to risk and taking chances. However, writing a book was different for me. Although I had my husband's full support, it was something I could only do on my own. It was completely terrifying for me to me to believe that it was remotely possible.

Several things needed to happen before I was finally able to pursue my dreams. One of the biggest factors that inspired me to take action came after I read *The Millionaire Messenger* by Brendon Burchard (Morgan James Publishing, 2011). It was as though Brendon was speaking directly to me when he wrote about "my message being bigger than me." It was at that moment that I was able to find perspective and understand why my dream meant so much to me. For me, my dream is to make a difference in the lives of others. I would do anything to be able to help someone find *hope* during his or her darkest moments. My message was not about me; it was about honoring my purpose. Discovering this allowed me to focus on *why I wanted to help others so desperately*. Once I fully understood my "why," there was no looking back.

I still had to reconcile another piece within myself. Before I could put my best effort into writing a book, I needed to be willing to step fully into my light. By that I mean I had to let go of my fear of shining and allow myself to become everything my soul was capable of being. I had to graciously and fully accept the gifts I was about to share with the world. Wow, talk about frightening! Once I became focused on my "why" and was ready to step fully into my light, I was not willing to let fear stand in my way.

Only then was I ready to strategize and make a plan of action. I knew it was going to take some time if I was going to give it my best effort. I dedicated two to three days a week to furthering my studies. I spent hours researching experts and coaches who were bestselling authors, publishers, and marketing gurus. I devoted the following year to enrolling in online classes and programs that taught me everything that I would need to know before I got started writing my book.

During that year, I began to gain a clear vision of what my book would be about and the audience I wanted to reach. I was blessed to receive guidance and coaching from several *New York Times* bestselling authors and coaches, to whom I owe my deepest gratitude. This guidance gave me the foundation and the tools necessary to take action.

Dreams can come true. Know your why. Listen to it. Fully accept your gifts and step into your light. Make a plan and take action. The authentic desires that lie within your soul can't be silenced. They will remain with you until you answer their call.

Take action.

1. Are you *interested* in achieving your dreams, or are you *committed*? Interest will merely entertain your thoughts. Making a commitment to take action will greatly increase your odds of attaining your goals. Real change requires commitment and action.

2. Know your why. It is at the core of whether you will take action or not. If you do not really have a strong why, your desire will most likely remain just a dream.

3. If you are ready to put in place a plan of action, start small. For example, if your dream is to move to another city or faraway location and you have not been there before, plan a trip. At the very least, learn everything you can about its cost of living, culture, business, and lifestyle by doing research online.

4. Set a date for meeting your goal. Write it down. By declaring your intention and setting a date, you are committing yourself to achieving it. Share your plans with others.

5. Start to make mini goals. These are goals that you will commit yourself to daily, weekly, or monthly in order to meet your desired end result. For example, within two weeks, you will list your home on the market. You will start saving an extra $500 a month towards moving expenses. You will network with other people who have your desired expertise or skills to help you with your career.

6. Once you create a clear, well-thought-out plan and take the necessary action towards achieving your goals, your path will start to unfold and lead you in your desired direction.

Conclusion

Discover the Magic of the Unexpected Journey

You have a clean slate every day you wake up. You have a chance every single morning to make that change and be the person you want to be. You just have to decide to do it. Decide today's the day. Say it: this is going to be my day.

—Brendon Burchard

Every day you have a new opportunity to create the life you desire. This sacred gift is seldom recognized and less often taken. My wish for you today is that you will decide to begin living the life you truly desire *this moment*, regardless of any adversity or challenges you may be facing. Believe you can do it. It is not too late.

Some of the happiest and most successful people on earth have gone through unimaginable struggles and heartache. The joy and unexpected blessings came *after* they learned to accept their circumstances and express gratitude for everything they already had.

Life is not perfect, and seldom is it easy. However, its hidden beauty and greatest treasures often lie in its imperfections and struggles. Life is nothing more, nor less, than a series of moments. These moments are defined only by the meaning we give them. Even when horrible things happen that greatly affect our well-being, even in these moments, we have the opportunity to have hope, to look beyond this single moment and have faith that, in time, this difficult moment will enable a future joy and happiness that could never have been possible without it.

My life has taught me that what seems impossible can become possible. To reflect on the extraordinary journey of my forty-seven years of life leaves me breathless. I am in awe of the miracles I have witnessed numerous times in my life—especially the ones that came when I was on the brink of giving up. And the same can be true for you. Let my life serve as proof that you should *never* give up. I thank God every day for giving me the strength and faith to go on.

If you have ever believed that adversity was a punishment or a curse, I hope that paradigm has now been shattered. Adversity is what opens the doors of possibility in your life and allows you to create more happiness than you could ever fathom. It empowers you to discover the hidden gifts already present in your life, perhaps still buried beneath layers of pain and hurt. My wish is for you to look back on your journey, which may feel so difficult now, and know that within it lies a seed for which nothing but miracles, abundance, and joy can grow—without changing a single circumstance.

If you have come this far on our journey together, I can only assume that you too have dreams in your heart that you wish to bring to life. No matter how small or grand they are, honor them. Acknowledge their existence. Reflect on their significance in your journey. Connect with the passions within you that ignite your soul.

And if you have been suffering or unhappy, decide now to make the switch from surviving to thriving. Create more of what you desire in your life. Start loving your life and living passionately. With the right mindset, along with the new tools you have discovered, you too can create a life filled with joy and abundance.

Today, as I come to the end of another chapter in my life, I know that the universe is preparing me for yet another beautiful new beginning, as I embrace my own gift of intuition more and more. Although some things in my life slightly resemble my past, much change has occurred within me. No longer am I lost and afraid of the days that lie ahead. I now have confidence and excitement, knowing that, with change, new opportunities will come. No matter what the future holds, I have learned that all I will ever need to know for my journey ahead already exists within me.

Your intuition is one of your greatest gifts as well. Embrace this gift. Learn to recognize its voice. Trust that once you are able to hear it, it will steer you on a path toward happiness and abundance. Never again fear it, or the power that exists within your soul.

By now you know the GOLD nuggets I have collected along my journey. I discovered them only after learning to surrender to the detours of my life and having faith these challenges would take me to a place of wonder that would illuminate my being. May these nuggets be a catalyst for your transformation. In fact, all of these gifts can be summed up in a single GOLD nugget of their own:

Discover the hidden   **G**ifts beneath the challenges you face.

Become empowered: **O**wn your actions and take control of your life.

Find true happiness: **L**ove yourself by letting go of negative beliefs.

Create a life you truly   **D**esire: Life is beautiful, so choose to live beautifully.

Thank you for sharing this time with me. If you would like to continue on this journey together and join the movement of women discovering how to let the beauty unfold in their lives, please visit my website at http://www.beautyunfoldingbook.com. (While you are there, make sure to claim your free gift!) Whether through mentorship programs, live events, or retreats I welcome the opportunity to get to know you.

Decide that today is the day of your beautiful new beginning, and let your beauty unfold.

Acknowledgments

With love and gratitude:

To my mentors, Brendon Burchard, Peggy McColl, and Christine Kloser—thank you for sharing your wisdom and insight as bestselling authors, and helping me to find the courage to share my message with the world.

To Amanda Rooker, my wonderful editor, and her team at SplitSeed. I am so grateful not only for your guidance and encouragement, but also for opening your heart to the story I want to share with others.

To David Hancock at Morgan James Publishing—thank you for believing in me and my vision for my book. I also want to thank the team at Morgan James Publishing, especially Terry Whalin, Rick Frishman, Jim Howard, Bethany Marshall, and Margo Toulouse, for helping me with my entire publishing process.

To my spiritual guides and mentors, especially Simon James, Brenda Lawrence, Anne Reith, and Cheryl Breaker. I am forever grateful to you for helping me to awaken and discover the spiritual gifts within me. It has blessed my life in more ways than I could ever have imagined.

Thank you to all of my dear friends, especially Nicole Catalano, Laura Roche, and Laura Corsetti—you are all treasures in my life! Nicole, my soul sister, I can't imagine my life without you or your love and friendship. Even though we may live thousands of miles apart, you are always close to my heart. Thank you for always being there to love and support me through of all life's highs and lows. To my dearest friend Laura Roche, I adore you. Thank you so much for the gift of your friendship. I know I can bare my soul to you and you would never judge me. I can always count on your wisdom, honesty, love, and support. You have blessed my life in more ways than I could ever say. And to Laura Corsetti, my lifetime friend. I am so grateful for the forty years of love and friendship we have shared. Even though we live many miles away, I can always count on your love and concern. Your love and caring is one of the greatest blessings in my life.

To my beautiful nieces Kylie, Ally, Ava, and Sam—thank you for putting a smile in my heart. I love and adore you.

To my mom and dad, Joan and Walter Grotz—your love and support means more than words can say. Mom, thank you for encouraging me to write this book. Dad, thank you for always reminding me to savor the *lemonade* in my life. I am truly blessed to have you both as parents. I love you dearly.

To my daughter Chelsea—thank you for all of your honest feedback, encouragement, expertise, and the hundreds of other ways you supported me, but most of all for your love. You are an extraordinary writer and publicist—you have so many gifts to share with the world! I am so fortunate to have you by my side. I am incredibly blessed to have you for a daughter.

To my son Carter—I am continually in awe of your wisdom, hard work and fierce determination. Your gifts as a natural leader, a powerful speaker and chief -motivator inspire me every day! I am so grateful for all of your love, support and encouragement.

To my (self-proclaimed) favorite child, Cooper—thank you for being so incredibly understanding of the countless hours I spent writing this book. You make me feel like the luckiest person on the planet when you celebrate my successes! Your wit, humor, and compassion always make me smile and warm my heart.

To my husband Mark—thank you for always believing in me even when I doubted myself. Your unwavering support and love have given me the freedom and the gift to go after my dreams. I am in awe of your determination, strength, and mental fortitude. Your ability to overcome obstacles in life and to reach goals many would believe to be impossible empowers me to live life boldly. Thank you for the millions of ways you show your love for me every day. My love for you and our family is endless.

About the Author

Kate Waite has mastered the art of living beautifully, even after enduring several devastating events in her life. After being severely burned in a fire at age fifteen, Kate became more determined than ever to find the beauty in life. Over the last thirty years, through trial, tests, and self-discovery, Kate has found that the secret to living a beautiful life is to create joy and abundance from within. Before becoming an author, Kate found success as a self-taught fashion designer, whose designs were featured on *ABC News*, *Good Morning America*, and *All My Children*. Today she is passionate about "paying it forward" and helping to empower women to live their most beautiful lives through her gifts as an author, inspirational speaker, and lifestyle expert. As a first-time author, she was awarded a top honor and prize in the 2012 Transformational Author Writing Contest for her submission *Gifts God Gives*.

To learn more about Kate, go to:

http://www.beautyunfoldingbook.com.

You can follow her on:

- Facebook: http://www.facebook.com/beautyunfoldingbook
- Twitter: https://twitter.com/thelifeyoudream
- Instagram: @LivingBeautifullyNow

Resources

National Toll-Free Numbers for Additional Help
Drug & Alcohol Treatment Hotline: 1-800-662-HELP
Domestic Violence Hotline: 1-800-799-7233
Domestic Violence Hotline/Child Abuse: 1-800-4-A-CHILD
(1-800-422-4453)
Rape, Abuse, and Incest National Network: 1-800-656-HOPE
(1-800-656-4673)
Eating Disorders Center: 1 -800-236-1188
Self-Injury: 1-800-DONT CUT (1-800-366-8288)*
Note: NOT a crisis line. This is for information and referrals only.

Printed in the USA
CPSIA information can be obtained
at www.ICGtesting.com
JSHW082338140824
68134JS00020B/1749

9 781630 474409